May you always have the treasures of His words! ♡ - Brooke

WORDS

ARE

TREASURES

BROOKE RICK

D1360362

To Anthony, for always holding my hand and pointing me to Jesus.

To my Three—Silas, Ezra, and Ruby, you give me hope for a better future.

To Mom and Dad, for everything, but especially for teaching me how to contend in prayer.

To Alyssa and Austin, for being a triple cord and always being brave for one another.

*To Jason and Raina Byars, for taking a chance on two kids, and because,
"If you don't quit, you can't lose."*

*To Barbara Lamberth, Donna McNulty, and Laura Fadden, for loving me as if I was
your own. You became mine and have impacted me more than I could ever say.*

Above all, this is for Jesus, My King.
*You are my All in All. Please use this obedience to teach others that they can hear
Your Voice and have the treasures of Your Words.*

CONTENTS

FOREWORD

When I first met Brooke, I immediately knew she was someone special. She was knowledgeable, driven, and possessed a wealth of wisdom beyond her years. As we dated and eventually married, it was (and still is) a tremendous honor to stand by her side and proudly declare, "She has a way with words!" Whether posting on Instagram, writing a birthday card to a family member, or scribbling a note of encouragement to a friend—she and I could sit down with the same writing task, and yet you'd quickly see her words stand out with eloquence, grace, and authenticity while mine show a struggle to hammer out a couple of mediocre sentences in an attempt to express what I feel in my heart.

When we first moved to Florida to be youth pastors, Brooke and I hosted a youth group in our home. Even in those days, with just a handful of students circled up in our living room, I often pushed off the teaching segment of the meeting to her since she, after all, was the qualified teacher and the one with the best words. God has really stretched me over the years, and though I still get just as nervous speaking in front of people, I can confidently say that I still could not do what I do without my wife!

Even now, as I've grown in my role and gifting as a pastor and communicator, I still go to her with my notes and outlines for advice, ideas, and even correction because I truly value her input. We absolutely work as one, yet oftentimes, I will be the one on a platform in front of people attempting to communicate the timeless truth of the Gospel. I guess what I'm trying to say is this: If you've heard me, you've heard Brooke.

Our pastor, Jason Byars, often says, "I've got nothing good to say outside of God's Word." I'll echo that, but I also feel that in most cases, I've got nothing good to say without passing it through the Brooke-filter first. When she first told me that she felt God's leading to write a book, I was so excited because I know this book is going to reach just the right people with just the right words at just the right time. Her words will definitely encourage others to become treasure seekers.

Our kids have their own little treasure box on their desks. The contents range from random coins, shells found at the beach, rocks dug up on a hike, and little toys and trinkets that have some sort of significance to them. What most people would see as random or worthless, they see as prized possessions and cherished possessions. You might think that your life, your story, your experiences are insignificant, nothing special, no big deal, blah, but God, Abba Father, sees these things as so important, so full of worth, so treasured.

You are holding in your hands a small treasure chest full of golden experiences and gems of wisdom in all shapes and sizes. The beauty is that on the surface, some of these words and moments may seem common, every-day, and ordinary. But when the Holy Spirit breathes on the ordinary, it's extraordinary! Furthermore, as you read these pages, I believe your eyes will open to the vast treasure-trove of your own life that you are already in possession of. Words are indeed treasures! The Word of God is alive, and your testimony needs to be written, spoken, and paired with the power of God's Word, so that other people can benefit from your wealth of experiences!

One of my all-time favorite movies is *Hook*. It's an interesting backstory on Peter Pan—if you haven't seen it, do yourself a favor and watch it tonight (after reading this book, of course!) One scene in the movie, the lost boys are trying to train Robin Williams' character to remember that he is actually Peter Pan! He forgot who he was once he left Neverland! He grew up.

Spoiler alert! There's a scene where they come to the end of a long, hard day of training, and Peter is exhausted. He smells dinner being prepared and he's visibly eager and excited to eat after the grueling workout he has endured. He sits down at the table and many covered dishes are brought out. Everyone is ready to eat! They say "grace" and open up the containers only for us to realize that once the steam clears, they are empty! Surprised, Peter sits back as he watches the lost boys scooping, grabbing, and full-on feasting on invisible food! The camera intentionally shows close-ups of the lost boys over-emphasizing each bite of invisible burgers and each nibble of invisible corn on the cob. Peter is extremely irritated. As the scene plays out, they move into a time of dogging each other with words; throwing cut-downs and insults back and forth as a game. Peter eventually gets so caught up into this game that he takes a spoon and scoops a big clump of nothing out of an empty bowl and catapults it at a lost boy, only to find that a bright colored blob of whipped dessert splats on the boy's face! As the lost boys look back at Peter in amazement, to his own surprise Peter now sees the table full of an unbelievable spread of food—a colorful variety of pies, smoking plates of meat, and all sorts of crazy looking entrées! The lost boys in unison begin to say something that still echoes in my head from time to time in different situations: "You're doing it! You're doing it, Peter!"

My prayer for you, dear reader, is that as you turn each page full of hidden treasures, you will begin to see what you didn't see before! I hope this book will inspire you to dig into the Word of God and discover some gold for yourself! As you read, you will be so encouraged by the words on these pages that you begin to experience the riches of His glory in your everyday life! I believe that as you gain eyes to see and ears to hear, in faith, you will hear that still small voice of the Holy Spirit and a great cloud of witnesses say: "You're doing it, Peter!"

—*Anthony Rick*
Coastline Community Church
Indian Harbour Beach, Florida

PREFACE
ALL IN FOR LOVE

don't know about you; but I'm all in for love. I always have been. My husband, Anthony, has told me that I love my extended family an unusual amount. Perhaps, it was my dad's *toda la familia* mantra that just was embedded into me. You mean, you don't talk to your mom, dad, sister, and brother every single day also? Anthony wasn't complaining because he also knew that I was the girl that he asked to be his girlfriend and stayed his girlfriend when three weeks later he told me that God was opening a door for him to move to Los Angeles. Being all in, and totally assured that God spoke to my heart that Anthony would be my husband, he moved across the country and I remained all in as we were long distance for sixteen months.

I need to pause to remind you that long distance in 2007 looked a lot different than today. There was no facetime, video recordings, or unlimited media storage. In fact, the cell phone carriers charged *per text* and your messages could only have 160 emoji-less characters. That was a lot of back spacing for an *in love* wordsmith like me. Oh, and him too. Another drawback was that your phone could only save 20 messages so I would think long and hard before deleting or choosing to save a love note. Long distance in the dark ages, included staying up really late (or for Anthony getting up really early) because we were two hours apart. It included intentional letter writing that you had to go to the store and purchase a stamp for. Sometimes long distance love was Anthony sending a gift or flowers, but not through Amazon because the Amazon that we know today didn't exist and there were no apps for smartphones. God was teaching us how to cultivate a love that was worthy of required effort. God was also teaching us about having assurance based on treasuring what He has spoken to our hearts even when circumstances are not what we are expecting.

An all in girl like me had to, of course, choose an all in guy like Anthony. You might think that I wanted a guy who would treat me well and be absolutely captivated by me. A guy who would match my love with his love. But that was not my primary aim. Before I met Anthony, I had sworn off dating because I was doing the worst job ever at finding a guy who aligned with who I was. What troubled me more was that I was having a really hard time knowing who I was apart from someone else. I didn't know what to look for. I decided to only pursue God for a set amount of time because I really loved Him and wanted to just enjoy being single and alone in relationship with Him.

At eighteen I poured out my heart and told God—*"God, I don't want to find someone else to be my first love. It's You. If I have something really sad happen, then I want to go to You and talk to You about it. If something really happy happens, then I want to share it with*

You first. God, I want to undividedly give myself to You and I'm trusting You to bring me the one that You have for me. In fact, I even want You to pick them out. I want them to be totally as in love and all in with You as I am. Maybe even more than that!" That year of aloneness with God was the one where I really began my relationship with Him. God became my joy, my love, my all in all. A year later, I met Anthony Rick, the one who I was told was untouchable and who dates no one. The one who I saw really, really loved God with his whole life.

After I graduated college, I eventually moved to Los Angeles too. All in and freshly inspired by Erin Gruwell and the *Freedom Writers,* my first job was teaching English classes in a rehabilitation school for teenagers who were getting their lives back on track from a variety of hard situations that often involved gangs, drugs, and broken homes. It was so good to finally be near Anthony, but sometimes I teased him that he was becoming a zombie. All in himself, Anthony spent most of his time that year living on airplanes or behind the drums. He was both an incredible drummer for a touring worship team, and a part of a church planting team in New York. The church planting team flew from LA to NYC each week to train up a permanent team, and to hold Monday night services in Manhattan. Anthony was definitely all in, too.

We were married the next summer and four months later we began to feel a need to transition from Los Angeles, California; and a stirring to help with a three-year-old church plant, all the way across the country in Melbourne Beach, Florida. There weren't too many who understood what we were feeling and why we were considering this move since we had never even considered moving to Florida and had never even been to the church plant. God began to tug on our hearts and tell us that He needed us there. He needed two faith-filled, wide-eyed newlyweds who wanted to be the hands and feet of Jesus and minister to people who had never experienced God's love. We gave God our requests, much like Gideon's fleece test, and said, *"If it is really You calling us, God, would You show us by doing three specific things?"* He answered us and filled us with peace and wonder. We were both all in. With blind faith the last week of October 2009, we packed our few belongings and our little puppy, Oso, in our red Mustang and told our friends goodbye. We drove from the coast of Santa Monica to a town we had never visited before on the coast of Melbourne Beach.

We joined a small team of church planters who set up and tore down all the chairs and equipment that was needed each week to hold church in a middle school cafeteria. We quickly became youth pastors, then church building fundraisers and renovators, and wore many other hats. When Anthony and I set out on this adventure, we had faith that might seem big, but it was still small in many ways. Thankfully, Jesus said all we need is faith the size of a mustard seed (Luke 17:6). Back then, my faith said, *"Let's just give it a year, we can commit to anything for a year."* Now, my faith has grown to an enduring faith and we have now been stubbornly planted for twelve years. In spite of trials and waiting periods, we have learned that we are in the will of God when we are positioning ourselves *to do* the will of God with hearts that desire to say *whatever You will, we will do it.*

I'm still the "all in with love" girl. All in with God. All in with Anthony. All in with my children—Silas, Ezra, and Ruby. All in with loving people and believing for them no matter how lost the situations seem. I know that many people think that being all in with love is scary. And as a recovered scaredy cat (more on that later), I think the reason that I can be all in with love is because I have learned to treasure God's words. His words give us confidence because, "He is not a man that He should lie." (Numbers 23:19), and they are always backed by His constant character. There is also an assurance that comes from knowing that God is close and mindful of us when we see the way He speaks to us in our day to day lives. That's why words from God are treasures. Treasures that reflect glory.

This book is a labor of love to give you permission *to wonder;* to be filled with surprise that God speaks to you in both the unexpected and the familiar. It is permission that you don't have to do anything to earn it or to obtain a certain amount of knowledge first, but that it's simply your right as a child of God to hear and treasure the words of your Father. This book is for the seeker, the curious, the humble, and the childlike. It is even for the one who doesn't feel like they can hear God. I hope whoever you are, this book comes across as if we have warm cups of coffee in hand and are sitting on my back porch sharing. I pray you feel full of peace and comfort as you listen to me tell you about the goodness of God and that I may declare the praises of Him who called me out of darkness into his wonderful light and that you might reflect on how He has called out to you too (1 Peter 2:9). Above all, I hope you are filled with desire and curiosity for God's word. Words are treasures.

NOTE

At the end of each chapter, I have included a **Prayer for the Seeker**. God promises, "You will seek me and find me when you seek me with all your heart." (Jeremiah 29:13) I invite you at the end of each chapter to linger—posture your heart and mind, pray, journal, and worship—this is seeking. You will also find a **Soaking Song** or **Songs** that might have been referenced in the chapter or because the song's words encapsulate the theme of the chapter. Soaking in worship means to wait on the Lord. It means to relax yourself in His presence and to become aware that He is near. Simply, soaking is to still yourself and to refrain from striving.

CHAPTER ONE

TREASURES

More than anything, Peter Mark Roget loved two things, making lists and words. Once he retired from his professional career, Peter's obsession was compiling extensive lists of related words. In 1852, his collection was published and he named his masterpiece, *Roget's Thesaurus*. Even today, the world knows the *Thesaurus* as a commonplace writing tool for finding the perfect word or discovering the most interesting synonym or antonym. However, most people don't know that the name Thesaurus was chosen by Roget for his lexicon because of it's greek meaning—*storehouse of precious jewels*. For a lover of words like myself, this makes my heart sing! It feels incredibly romantic and like the perfect hidden truth that only a wordsmith would know! All of me says, *"Good job, Roget! You nailed it! Yes, words are treasures!"*

Have you ever thought about how words are like treasures? Finding the perfect word in writing might be the crown jewel of your sentence! There might be a favorite book on your shelf with opening lines that transport you to another place or time. A quote with an image that you have to share with others because it sums up exactly how you feel. Whether or not you are a lover of words makes no difference; we can agree that words, especially written words, have weight and can be timeless. Long after the author has passed, the words penned live on forever. Perhaps, the way that writing can immortalize thoughts in the world is what inspires me the most. Words are treasures.

Of all the words in the world, my most cherished ones come from God. Words of purpose. Words eternal. Words from the Name of Above All, the Ancient of Days. Words that Abba left for me and you. Over time as I've grown closer to God, I have fallen so in love with my Bible, His written words. When I think about the brave people who have risked or given their lives to take God's Word to places where it isn't available, I feel so unbelievably blessed. When I hear the stories of the countless individuals who only have one tangible page torn from a Bible and the way that they have memorized every word so that it stays in their heart forever where no one could take it away from them; I feel so undeserving to possess multiple Bibles in various formats and translations.

The value of God's Word is exceedingly greater than any other treasure we might find! The collection of His Words is a storehouse of riches, themselves, just like Roget called his *Thesaurus*. All throughout the Bible, there are references of different kinds of storehouses. God asks Job if he knows where the storehouse of snow is. In Malachi, He tells Israel to bring the whole tithe to the storehouse. Storehouses of wind are spoken about in Jeremiah and storehouses of the sea are found in the

Psalms. How wild is it to think that God, Creator of All, has storehouses! Deuteronomy 28:12 says, "The Lord will open for you His good storehouse, the heavens, to give rain to your land in its season and to bless all the work of your hand; and you shall lend to many nations, but you shall not borrow." His good storehouse! The Amplified Bible calls it His good treasure house. One day, the Holy Spirit reminded me, "*Words are treasures.*"

In my mind's eye, I picture large silos, like the ones that hold grain, but they are filled to the brim with pages written in the most beautiful gold, sparkling ink. I look through them and written on the pages are promises and words of God. Treasured verses from the Bible that I cling to. These words are *logos* words. *Logos* refers to the general words of the Bible that are for all believers. *Logos* in Greek and Hebrew refer to the Word of God. In this storehouse, I see so many treasures because God is always speaking through *logos*, for His Word is living! As I sift through the treasured papers, I notice that written on some pages are words that feel more specific to me. These precious words are *rhema* words. *Rhema* words are logos words that the Holy Spirit illuminates to a seeking heart. It is very important to know that *logos* and *rhema* are always in alignment with one another. *Rhema* is backed by *logos*. These words that speak to one's heart are inspired words from the Holy Spirit that are always in agreement with God's written Word.

The Apostle Paul spoke about *rhema* words in Romans 10:17 when he said, "So then faith comes by hearing, and hearing by the word (*rhema*) of God." When your mind and spirit are quickened by God's Word, and you know that you hear God speak to you on a matter, it produces faith. Faith sparked from *hearing* the Word that God *is* speaking. *Rhema* words are faith producing words that God speaks directly to you; scripture that is energized and revealing about your specific situation and what you need to know in your "knower" in that very moment. This is why you may hear the same message from God's Word in a room full of people, but it completely changes everything just for you. It feels like the entire sermon is for you and you alone.

This storehouse of my heart is filled with pages that have treasures of *logos* and also the riches of *rhemas* that God has spoken directly to my heart. I picture these written in my handwriting because I have personally heard, meditated on, and written them down. Many of them tearstained because I have embraced them as my personal source of hope during the darkest of nights. Some fill me with joy because they are shouts of victory and answered prayers penned on the mountain tops of life! Others are reminders of verses that have come alive at specific times in my life. All of them, full of imagery that He has placed in my mind's eye. These treasures are daily words that my Father spoke to my heart in the secret place.

Psalm 91:1 says, "He that dwelleth in the secret place of the most High shall abide under the shadow of the Almighty." Jesus instructed us, "But when you pray, go into your room and shut the door and pray to your Father who is in secret. And your Father who sees in secret will reward you." (Matthew 6:6) The secret place is where I meet with my Father and where He sees me and gives rewards. The rewards of His precious answers (*rhema*) on the matters of my heart. His Word, His treasures, jewels from His storehouse now fill my storehouse! If I'm His temple, His house of prayer, then I'm adorned with gems of *rhema*! God still speaks; and if we position ourselves in a place of prayer, we can hear the treasures of His words.

When I refer to words as treasures, it is not because they are big or fancy. In fact, to you, they might just be ordinary. These words that are in my storehouse sparkle like gems because of the value they hold to me. I can point to them and say, "Let me tell you about this one!" I can thoughtfully choose a specific, treasured word—from the many I've collected while walking with my Father—and

> GOD STILL SPEAKS; AND IF WE POSITION OURSELVES IN A PLACE OF PRAYER, WE CAN HEAR THE TREASURES OF HIS WORDS.

share it with someone in need. That is testimony! These show-and-tell-treasures increase the wonder of anyone who hears, and help us recall the faithfulness of our Father! I'm reminded that Paul spoke of the beautiful word of their testimony, when he said, "Remember, our Message [*Words,* substitution mine] is not about ourselves; we're proclaiming Jesus Christ, the Master. All we are is messengers, errand runners from Jesus for you. It started when God said, 'Light up the darkness!' and our lives filled up with light as we saw and understood God in the face of Christ, all bright and beautiful. If you only look at us, you might well miss the brightness. We carry this precious Message around in the unadorned clay pots of our ordinary lives." (2 Corinthians 4 MSG) What if the words that God gives us in His Word, in the secret place, are the treasures we possess in earthen jars? We are those jars! When we, who once were lost in darkness are filled with God's light, become transformed into storehouses, ourselves! We are carriers of the words of our testimony—the testimony of Jesus!

Did you know that God still speaks and that you can hear the voice of God? This is a part of the original design in the Garden of Eden. Adam spent time walking and talking with God in the cool of the day. Each day man would commune with the God of all. This models the close relationship God desires to have with you. Have you ever considered that it is *possible* to hear God daily? Hearing God and taking hold of the words He has for you is the truest of treasures! The richest of riches! The Message translation of 1 Kings 3:9 says that the wisest king to ever live said that the one thing that he desired was a *"God-listening heart."* Solomon knew he could hear and listen to God. It is the great pearl to be sought! If we want to hear Him, we need to stay close to His Presence.

For many of us, we are so good at following the principles of religion, the principles of Christianity, or morality, or the principles of being a good person...but do you *know* His voice? When you pray, do you hear His answers? "Whether you turn to the right or to the left, your ears will hear a voice behind you, saying, '*This is the way; walk in it.*'" (Isaiah 30:21) Perhaps, knowing about God and knowing what we've heard or what we've sung keep us just at the door of His storehouse. Friend, enter in!

{ WHEN YOU PRAY, DO YOU HEAR HIS ANSWERS? } Enter into His good storehouse, to the Heavens, to the secret place, and take hold of the sparkling jewels that have your name on them! Gems intended just for you, about your future, about your children, about your dreams, and your cares! Oh, He cares for you! Don't you know He has something to say about all of the things? He is so very close!

The purpose of writing about these stories and revelations is to share some precious treasures that I've gathered along the way. They aren't just picked up and tossed, but thoughtfully considered and written on my heart. Perhaps, what I gather and call beautiful is something you might call a weed. Maybe not a weed that should be despised and plucked out; but certainly not of any importance. There is a saying among gardeners that, "It is soil if you want it and it is dirt if you don't." Wildflower or weed? Soil or dirt? Treasure or ordinary? When we give God the soil of our lives, the ordinary becomes holy, set apart, and full of value! Do you want to give God every area of your life so that the soil can hold beauty? I don't know about you, but I want to have a heart where revelation grows from cherishing every word. Some only hold value in what sounds lofty or grand or coming from someone that fits that description themselves. But I am reminded, "God chose the foolish things of the world to shame the wise; God chose the weak things of the world to shame the strong. God chose the lowly things of this world and the despised things—and the things that are not—to nullify the things that are, so that no one may boast before him. It is because of him that you are in Christ Jesus, who has become for us wisdom from God—that is, our righteousness, holiness and redemption. Therefore, as it is written: 'Let the one who boasts boast in the Lord.'" (1 Corinthians 1:27-31)

Maybe that which is lowly, simple, and childlike is the richest of all. The wisdom of God is foolishness to the world. Our boast is in the God of all who is in all and cares about it all! It is my hope, as you read these pages from the ordinary parts of my life, that your heart might burn deep within and find revelation in the pages of your life too. Words are treasures. The child of God is a storehouse of words, both past and present, and knows that there is more treasure in the future! Words that need to be shared for we overcome by the blood of the lamb and the word of our testimony. (Revelation 12:11) May these words of my heart spark hope in you and a desire to unlock the everyday riches of meditating on the words that God speaks.

"For where your treasure is, there your heart also will be."
Matthew 6:21

CHAPTER TWO

A FRIEND IN JESUS

grew up with parents that pointed me to Jesus. I feel like I have loved him from the very beginning. This isn't a small thing—it's a miracle that I can truly appreciate now that I'm older with children of my own. My parents were raised in loving homes, but their childhoods did not have a home like the one that I grew up in. The home, by grace and grace alone, I got to grow up in was filled with love, yes, but what defined it more was the peace of God that stretched wall-to-wall and from the floor to the top of the ceiling. I have to believe this peace came into our family when the two, fresh-out-of-high-school, young adults made the decision to let Jesus become the centerpiece of their marriage. No, they weren't perfect. Yes, there was yelling and the kind of arguments that should be expected when two barely-twenty-year-olds, who know nothing but think they may know everything, get married and try to pave their way. Despite the odds being against them in every way, there was a friendship that they both had with Jesus, the Prince of Peace. There's a song from Hillsong Young & Free that says "peace is a promise He keeps," and a verse in John Chapter 14 where Jesus says that He leaves peace with us and the peace that He gives is not like the world. The Amplified version of this verse says, "Let My perfect peace calm you in every circumstance and give you courage and strength for every challenge." My parents had this peace because of their friendship with Jesus, and no matter the circumstances of finances, health, heartache, or choices; they had strength and courage.

There's a spiritual principle of sowing and reaping, and because my parents sowed in their relationship with Jesus, their children became happy recipients of a friendship with Jesus from their earliest days. I didn't have an issue distinguishing between the Easter Bunny and the Tooth Fairy and Jesus. My upbringing provided the scaffolding that taught me that Jesus was different. Jesus was a man that was historically factual, and a relationship with him was experientially actual. The other guys, like Santa Claus, were fun and make-believe, but Jesus? I knew Him! This was not conditioning, but this was a relationship that grew from nighttime prayers, from devotions modeled, and prioritizing going to church from my earliest years. When I became a teenager, I suddenly realized there were many directions that I could go. One way was the wide road with the popular crowds and loads of options. Though this way was tempting, there always seemed to be my friend, Jesus, calling me to a less travelled road.

It was in those years that I chose Him for myself. It wasn't out of duty to my upbringing, but out of the delight of friendship. In high school my alarm would go off at 5:50 am, providing me enough time for a quick shower and plenty of time to sit on the floor before my mirror getting ready. My house would be so quiet because only I, who my dad would tease, "had people to impress," required the necessary thirty plus minutes of getting-ready time before I grabbed a piece of toast and ran to the car to get to school at 6:50 am. (Can you believe my school started at 7:15 in the morning?) Those thirty minutes started with putting in my favorite worship song into my cd player on repeat—one song that would play again and again becoming the words of the worship that was in my heart. Something like, *"Better is one day in your courts, better is one day in your house than a thousand elsewhere..."* Quietly, I would pray and talk to Jesus, and He didn't seem the least bit put off that I was curling my hair and putting on my makeup. He would fill my heart with peace and courage. Even if sometimes I felt scared about going to school because of how taxing all the different social situations were on my introverted heart; or because I was remembering Cassie Bernall from Columbine, who was killed for her faith, and having read her journal, realized how so much of me was like so much of her. Even when my heart felt uneasy, or I felt lonely, I knew Jesus went with me. If I was alone, I knew I was alone with Him.

> WHEN YOU CHOOSE JESUS, YOU GET GRAFTED INTO THE FAMILY OF GOD! YOU GET ACCESS TO FRIENDSHIP AND CLOSENESS.

My friendship with Jesus, the greatest of all treasures, was part of my inheritance that my parents chose for me. (Pay attention to that, parents!) Even so, there was still a required personal responsibility to take hold of what my parents had spent years praying into for me. I will be forever thankful for their leading me to my own relationship with Jesus; but I can't help but think of people who didn't grow up in a home like mine.

I'm filled with compassion for people that know of Jesus, or maybe they attend church; but it wasn't something they were intentionally led to. It was something they had to seek out on their own, and maybe they have never realized that they also can have this inheritance of closeness with Jesus. When these people think of their inheritance, it is something that resembles chaos or not knowing what actual love looks like. They feel like they must work so hard if they are ever going to amount to anything because the only one that they can depend on is themselves. I can't help but think that feeling like that has to feel so scary because we all know how often we let ourselves down. This inheritance feels like hopelessness or like a one in a billion chance at happiness, but certainly is not the way of peace.

When I think about these children of God, who just don't know about things like inheritance; I can hear the voice of my Friend, Jesus, saying in the very first verse of John 14, "Do not let your hearts be troubled"! I have the best news for you! When you choose Jesus, you get grafted into the family of God! You get access to friendship and closeness. *Family rights!* A new inheritance because now you are where you belong—where you belonged all along!

I love how Romans 8:17 reads in The Message!

This resurrection life you received from God is not a timid, grave-tending life. It's adventurously expectant, greeting God with a childlike "What's next, Papa?" God's Spirit touches our spirits and confirms who we really are. We know who He is, and we know who we are: Father and children. And we know we are going to get what's coming to us—an unbelievable inheritance! We go through exactly what Christ goes through. If we go through the hard times with Him, then we're certainly going to go through the good times with Him!

Some versions trade the word inheritance for treasure. Relationship with Jesus is the greatest treasure in the storehouse. It is the open door to all treasures and the way to hear His cherished words.

INHERITANCE

Do you feel like you are living with the revelation that you are *in* the family of God? Do you know that you are chosen and that you have full access to God, and full access to an inheritance both in heaven and on earth as it is in heaven? Maybe you struggle with being able to approach God as a Father or Jesus as a friend. The whole idea may seem impossible sometimes, because in your life it just hasn't played out like that. Let me encourage you that you do, in fact, have access to a close relationship with Jesus. It is your right, as a child of God. If you have cried out to God to rescue you, He has! Romans 10:13 tells us that, "All who call on the name of the Lord will be saved." Not all who call and who meet these conditions. No, it says—**"All who call on the name of the Lord will be saved."** Every mouth that calls on the name of the Lord, the name of Jesus Christ, will be saved.

Saved...
Written in...
Family...
Inheritance!

If Jesus is your Lord, He can be *yours*. I am my Beloved's and He is mine. It doesn't matter if your start was like my parents and all the odds were stacked against you and you don't really feel like anyone led you. I want to tell you that you were led by the pursuing love of the Father, the Son who made a way, and the Holy Spirit who illuminated that to you. It doesn't even matter if you had an upbringing that led you to Jesus and in foolishness you strayed and now you don't feel worthy. You need to know that you are worthy because you're wanted. The high price for salvation was paid, whether or not you would ever choose Him, because that's how much you are worth. You are beloved. I pray that the revelation that *Jesus is yours,* would sink deep into the fibers of who you are. He is your Lord, your Ally, your Friend, and your Beloved. May this revelation sink deep in the recesses of your body, mind, and soul.

A SEEKING PRAYER

Jesus, thank you for the treasure of being your friend! Thank you that You are not a distant, far off God, but a God who came to your people. Thank you that You still come to us! Jesus, we want to do life with You. Every day, every moment, please enter in and lead us! Please, help us to know You and to know Your voice, like sheep who know their Shepherd. Every lie or thought about You that isn't true, reveal it to us, so that we might know You in the ways that You actually are! Jesus, You're better than we thought! Thank you for coming to us, thank you for the riches of Your words!

SOAKING SONGS

Friend like Jesus by Steffany Gretzinger / Talking to Jesus feat. Brandon Lake

CHAPTER THREE

THE FORGIVING FATHER

n 2020, most of the world was in a quarantined state that was constantly referred to as *the most unprecedented time*. COVID-19 became a worldwide problem that caused my state to issue a safer at home policy for 30+ days. The safer-at-home idea continued on much longer than anyone could have anticipated. This concept ended up impacting the entire year of 2020—much greater than the 30+ day April mandate. It closed all social gatherings, and indirectly meant our church couldn't meet in it's typical ways of daily ministry to our community.

Our staff had to get creative to further meet the needs of our congregation through an online presence and ways with limited physical contact. It was amazing to see the testimonies that came out of the online community. Isolated people, who may have never felt comfortable to step foot into any church's door, were hearing the gospel come to them through their computers and phones. They could have been states away, some even in COVID hot spots, but were being connected to a pastor who prayed for them and offered hope right in their homes.

In 2020, I saw the collective body of Christ fearlessly and strategically reaching in—to meet with the lost, the scared, and the hurting. Throughout the COVID pandemic, there was a part of the church's heart that was left grieving as the body was

> WRESTLING WITH FEELINGS, TRADITIONS, AND PRIORITIES IS A GOOD AND NECESSARY THING.

so disconnected from each other and had so many obstacles in reaching out to others. There were feelings of just not being capable in the forced pause because we knew, without doubt, that there were so many who were hurting, needing, and suffering alone.

I began to learn that wrestling with feelings, traditions, and priorities is a good and necessary thing. It causes a reordering and an anticipation for a spiritual shift. It's seasons like this that teach you what "tried by fire" really means. When all was consumed, what remained? What was eternal? In that season, the grieving heart also became a hungry heart that said, *"Nothing else will satisfy except You, God! Whom shall I fear? I seek You and want to dwell in Your house all the days of my life!"* I can only imagine the unique ways that the seeking and desperate hearts of 2020 were answered by the Holy Spirit and drawn into the deeper places of hearing His voice! Because I know that when we call on Him, He answers! (Jeremiah 33:3)

Early on in this season, God gave me a dream where I was speaking with a friend who doesn't have a relationship with Jesus. In this dream, my friend called me while I was at church alone (with the exception of the streaming team) and she said, "Hey I heard that your church is doing some things for kids right now. Do you think you could come and do something with mine?" I left that empty service knowing that this was the most important ministry that I could do. This friend had never ever asked me to bring anything church-like to her children. This was the exact kind of testimony we were constantly hearing in that time—distant hearts now becoming wide open!

The dream continued, and I ended up at her house with some activities from our children's ministry and I asked her if this was okay. She replied, "Yes, I'm at my wit's end and this is great. Anything." I said, "Maybe we could play some music? It is worship, though?" I delicately tried to wade through the waters of the atmosphere. My friend then said, "Oh yes, that's fine, we are down with Jesus. He was a great person like other men of other faiths. Jesus, I don't have a problem with, but it's just God I have a hard time with." She waved her hands around dramatically as she said, "God." She went on to explain that, "The Christian God seems harsh and angry and not approachable." When she said these things to me, my heart softened and I explained to her, "That's because you know God abstractly, but when you know Him as Father, it changes how you view everything." With that I woke up.

Often when I have a dream that feels like it's the Lord downloading something into my heart, I lay in bed and talk to Him about it before my feet hit the ground. If I don't then the dream seems to vanish and so does any insight. When I asked the Holy Spirit about this dream, He reminded me of one of my favorite quotes by A.W. Tozer, "What comes into our minds when we think about God is the most important thing about us." He reminded me that so many don't know Him as Father. When Jesus spoke to God, He often called Him *Abba*. Abba, the word for father or papa or daddy. He didn't just refer to God as His Father, but called Him—*our* Father. Jesus tells us in John 14:6, "No one comes to the Father except through me." Through knowing Jesus, we can know the Father. Right after Jesus says this, the disciple Phillip asks Jesus to show them the Father. And Jesus answers him saying:

"Don't you know me, Philip, even after I have been among you such a long time? Anyone who has seen me has seen the Father. How can you say, 'Show us the Father?' Don't you believe that I am in the Father, and that the Father is in me? The words I say to you I do not speak on my own authority. Rather, it is the Father, living in me, who is doing his work. Believe me when I say that I am in the Father and the Father is in me." (John 14:9-11a)

We don't have to feel so bad when sometimes even the closest of Jesus' friends didn't understand either. Jesus tells us that we can know the character and personality of the Father because they are one, not separate from each other. So often theologies paint a picture, purposeful or not, that God is angry and fed up and sent His Son to get down here and fix things because we are never going to get it right.

Sometimes, we don't even see the Son rightly. We see Him say things in a way like, "Ugh, Phillip! When are you going to get it?" When I find myself reading things this way, I have to ask myself, *"But is that His nature?"* And I ask the Holy Spirit to reveal to me the treasure of His words. As we get closer and closer to Jesus, and treasure that relationship, we find we get closer and closer to the Father because they are One! And how did Jesus pray? John 17:11b, "Holy Father, keep

> JESUS SHOWS US HOW TO SEE THE FATHER RIGHTLY WHEN WE GET TO KNOW HIM, BECAUSE THEY ARE ONE.

them in your name, which you have given me, that they may be one, even as we are one." He desires for us to be so connected to Him and so connected to the Father, to Abba, that we are one with them! That doesn't sound one-sided to me. It doesn't sound self-serving or like patriarchy or someone who wants all that I can offer and holds back from me. No, the treasure of seeing the Father rightly is knowing He wants to be One with us. He wants us to have Him fully, and for us to also be fully given to Him. What an intimate, loving Father! Jesus modeled this by laying down his life, picking it up again and in doing so, made a way for all of us too! Jesus shows us how to see the Father rightly when we get to know Him, because they are One.

One of the parables that Jesus told that paints a picture of the Father was the story best known as the Prodigal Son. I've heard others say that it is more fitting to call it the "Running Father" because instead of turning away the son who squandered his inheritance; as soon as the father saw him, "while he was still a long way off", the father took off running to his son! The son didn't even get to explain himself before the father grabbed him and hugged him and kissed his neck! Then the dad, who had been watching the road for his son, threw a huge party celebrating his return, restoring him with a ring and a robe like he never lost the first inheritance. The image of this forgiving Father is the one that Jesus said our heavenly Father is like.

What a treasure to know that forgiveness and love to the fullest are characteristics of God. Doesn't it make you want to draw in close to Him? We can know that forgiveness is a characteristic of God because even in the Old Testament when Moses asked God what His name was; God responded, "Yahweh! The Lord! The God of compassion and mercy! I am slow to anger and filled with unfailing love and faithfulness. I lavish unfailing love to a thousand generations. I forgive iniquity, rebellion, and sin. But I do not excuse the guilty. I lay the sins of the parents upon their children and grandchildren; the entire family is affected—even children in the third and fourth generations." (Exodus 34:6-7 NLT)

His unfailing love to a thousand generations forgives iniquity, rebellion, and sin! That part sounds good, but when you read further about the "not excusing the guilty and laying sin on children and down through generations," it makes you want to hide under a rock! Hang with me though, it's worth it. We can't shy away from a forgiving God because certain verses seem scary. Those verses *are* scary. There are scary outcomes from remaining guilty and rejecting that "lavish-in-love" God who desires a relationship with you. If we accept the lavish-in-love part, the unfailing faithfulness, and the part about forgiving all the things, then we have to carry that knowledge into the next verse. What I mean is, we must know that *because* God is rich in love and unfailingly faithful, He *cannot* excuse the guilty. His goodness towards us does not allow it! If left in that state, the guilty would remain unhappy, unfulfilled, without peace, and settling for pig slop like the prodigal son. Our Father is too loving to allow that! He can't let the guilty remain guilty. It's too damaging to his sons and to his daughters. He deals with the root of sin completely so it doesn't have to pass through the generations. He deals with it so you can hand your children and grandchildren your victory of what God has delivered you from—instead of passing on to them your battles to also fight themselves. He removes the excuses, "It's the way my daddy was and his daddy was and it's the way you will be too." No, God desires to hand you the victory over your issues so that you can tell your children, "Others may battle this, but I fought it myself and I know the Lord as *my* deliverer. He is a strong tower and an ever present help! Whatever it is, it's not worth it, you don't even have to wonder. Child, you have tasted and seen that the Lord is good and you know it without doubt." He forgives iniquity, rebellion, and sin.

But if the guilty chooses to remain guilty, that loving God still wants to reveal the wages of sin to their children so that they might come to Him and call Him, "Abba!" Sin is held accountable so that the generations that follow will see it's worthlessness and discover that if they take one step to the Father, even if they don't see Him rightly yet, even if they are scared, or if they don't have a model of anyone showing them the way; they will find with one step, the forgiving Father will run the distance to scoop them up in His embrace! And if they harden their hearts and miss it, He will keep on trying—in the third generation, in the fourth generation! That is why some call this love wreckless and others call it unstoppable. It is why the religious just can't understand and don't know how to receive it or offer it. Who can fathom the treasure of knowing the forgiving and relentlessly loving Father? Paul calls it, "the spirit of adoption." This isn't a New Testament ideal, this is the consistent character of Yahweh.

MY DAD PURSUES ME WITH LOVE

This gem of the gospel is one of the most priceless ones to have. I so hope you say, "Oh this one is mine! I know that Father! He is mine and I am His!" Maybe you're not there yet and that's okay. Think about the thought, *God wants to be my dad.* Sometimes, our earthly fathers can ruin the very word—dad. But God is bigger and better than our greatest hopes of what a dad should or could be. Because He is not just dad, He is Yahweh, He is the Ancient of Days, He is the Alpha and the Omega and He pursues...you. *You!* He waits for you. He watches for you and watches over you. He isn't going to put you in a box and tell you that your life is going to be rigid and no fun. Have you thought that? What do you think of when you think of God? What does it say about how you see Him and what does it say about how you see yourself? Take some time today and think about just that...*what do I think of when I think of God?* This treasure is one that is too important to miss.

Stop right here...and think about Him.

God.

Yahweh.

Abba.

Now, with a heart that expects to hear, ask Him to reveal Himself to you. Wait in Presence and lean in with all your senses. What do you hear? What do you see? Journal your revelation.

A SEEKING PRAYER

Father, thank you for adopting us into Your family! Thank you for making a way. We see forgiveness, love, and faithfulness are parts of Your character that have never waivered. Forgive us for the times we have been too scared to approach You because we weren't seeing You rightly. God, we thought You would have been angry with us or that maybe You didn't want us because we didn't measure up. Thank you for Your loving-kindness that draws us to repentance. Thank you for cleansing us and not leaving us as sinners, but calling us sons and daughters. You are so, so kind. You are so good. Let us go about this day, in awe that the God of ALL loves us extravagantly.

A SOAKING SONG

Abba, I Belong to You by Jonathan David Helser

CHAPTER FOUR

HOLY SPIRIT, THE COMFORTER

J esus not only bears witness about our heavenly Father; He tells us about the Holy Spirit. In John 14:26, Jesus says, "The helper, the Holy Spirit, whom the Father will send in my name, will teach you everything. He will remind you of everything that I have ever told you." The Amplified version tells us that the Holy Spirit is our Comforter, Advocate, Intercessor—Counselor, Strengthener, and Standby, to represent and act on Jesus' behalf. A.W. Tozer talks about the Trinity in *The Knowledge of the Holy* and reminds that, "Every act of God is accomplished by the

> HOLY SPIRIT IS OUR COMFORTER, ADVOCATE, INTERCESSOR—COUNSELOR, STRENGTHENER, AND STANDBY, TO REPRESENT AND ACT ON JESUS' BEHALF

Trinity in unity. God does not divide Himself so that one Person works and another is inactive." Jesus tells us about the Father and the Father sent the Holy Spirit to dwell in us! In unity, all parts of the trinity pursue a relationship with the children of God.

The Holy Spirit lets us know that God is relational and near to us. Holy Spirit is the witness of the Father and the Son to us and He allows us to hear the voice of God. The Counselor helps us know God for ourselves, personally, not just what we've read or heard from others. A big part of our inheritance, as a part of the new covenant, is that every believer can and should hear the voice of God!

The Holy Spirit is our Comforter, our *parakletos*. Parakletos is the Greek word for intercessor, counselor, and advocate. One of the ways that the Holy Spirit gives us comfort is by speaking the Word of God to us. The Holy Spirit speaks to us the Word in the *logos* form on days that our devotion time is filled with exactly what we need to hear. Sometimes it may be a scripture that was shared on someone's social media and when we read it, the words energize and jump in our heart. The Holy Spirit may prompt your heart with a *rhema* whisper while you're driving in your car, or through the words of a stranger that edifies you or speaks clarity on something you've only been talking to God about. What a huge source of comfort it is to hear God for yourself on the matter! It puts strength in your heart to know that you are not alone and more importantly, that *you are known*. What you hear will be in unison with the promises of the Bible and will be consistent with God, who does not change.

We can gather comfort when the Holy Spirit reminds us that if God would consider Moses, His friend, I can be His friend too! If God answered David in his distress at Ziklag and said, "Surely he will recover everything," then I can hang on to the promise that I too, will recover anything that God intends for me! If it's not good yet, then God's not done! The Holy Spirit gives us courage by confirming what we know about God and by letting us know that He is with us.

"It shall come about after this that I shall pour out My Spirit on all mankind;
And your sons and your daughters will prophesy, Your old men will dream
dreams, Your young men will see visions. Even on the male and female
servants I will pour out My Spirit in those days."
(Joel 2:28-29)

The Holy Spirit doesn't just fill us with His presence, He also gives us the gifts and fruits of the Spirit. The gifts being—infilling, the gift and grace of speaking in other tongues, and also prophecy. This verse in Joel speaks about our present days and that all believers would have gifts of prophecy, dreams, visions, and experience God's Spirit. These things that prophet Joel mentioned are the gifts of the Spirit. In Acts, Chapter 2, we see the gift of the Holy Spirit come to the believers on the day of Pentecost. This day birthed the New Testament church and the culture carried on throughout all of Paul's writings! Paul tells us, "Pursue love, and earnestly desire the spiritual gifts, especially that you may prophesy." (1 Corinthians 14:18) Prophecy is speaking inspired words of the Holy Spirit. Sometimes, prophecy is for you, the Holy Spirit speaking God's word to you and giving you direction and answers. Other times, you may feel the Holy Spirit telling you something to share with another person in order that they might feel known by God and connected to Him. The Holy Spirit gives us words of treasure for ourselves and will also give us words for others.

Trust me, it isn't kooky! It may be as simple as a desire to check in on a friend and pray with them because they are on your heart. Maybe it is a prompting that you should share a specific scripture with someone. Sometimes though, Holy Spirit will specifically download something in your heart for a person and you will have a strong feeling that you need to share it with them. Feelings can be off at times because we are people and people are fallible. We can't be led by our feelings alone, but must grow in the discernment of the ways that God wants to use us. There's a humbleness that comes from checking in with God and knowing we need to rely on Him to bring about anything good. Conversely, we can not be so tied up in fear that we may be wrong or off, or think that it doesn't matter, that we keep to ourselves what God is speaking to our hearts. We need to know that we are in relationship with Him and *will hear* Him and know Him just like we know our friends. Our God can be known!

Most of my growth in the ability to hear God's voice has come from times that I have had to lean in intently, in order to know what His Word says, what His character reinforces, and how I can be obedient and know the next step I'm to take. These times where I really needed to have an answer have helped develop in me a posture of listening all the time. It isn't easy in today's world, and I often joke that my mind is like an Internet browser full of many tabs opened all at once. I have to make conscious decisions to cut through cluttered thoughts and to guard what I am consuming so that there is enough stillness to be able to listen. Sometimes there is so much going on that you can't hear a thing. When my mind begins to feel cluttered, or my heart feels anxious, that is a sign to me—*I am consuming too much.* When you find yourself in a place where you *have to hear,* it helps us create a space in ourselves to stay in a position that we are ready to hear. When life is moving along and things are just fine, I still want to hear God. The practice of listening to God when I really need to hear trains me to know how to hear at any time. An amazing by-product of having a God-listening heart is that sometimes we will hear God for others.

I'm a bit of an introvert at heart, so speaking to someone, especially if it is someone that I don't know very well, is terrifying! Especially, if you have only one spiritual impression and no idea what to say or do next. Anthony, my husband, explains it like this, "When the Holy Spirit shows us some-

> "SOMETIMES WE HOLD BACK SOME OF HEAVEN'S FRAGRANCE BECAUSE WE PUT A LID ON IT, AFRAID TO RELEASE TOO MUCH."

thing it's like a tissue box with only one tissue sticking out. If we reach and pull out that first tissue, another one pops up, and then another."

Sometimes, I have shied away from acknowledging an impression that seemed like it was for a person who was bagging my groceries or standing across the room for fear of being a weirdo or just completely off. Later on, I would find myself regretting it so much. What if by telling a young man wearing a nametag, Zachary, that the meaning of his name means "God remembers," unlocks something in his heart towards God? Maybe the Father remembers, but Zachary needed to know that God thinks about him and loves him. Why else would I have read the meaning of that name and on the same day only to later be face to face with a Zachary at the store? In *Dream Language: The Prophetic Power of Dreams,* Michal Ann Goll said, "Sometimes we hold back some of heaven's fragrance because we put a lid on it, afraid to release too much." When it was explained that way, revelation let loose something in me that knows that I can't hold back what heaven wants to release through me because there is a hurting world that needs it. I can't be afraid of releasing too much fragrance when there could be no better fragrance!

Last year, God placed a sweet and heartbroken older man in a small class of people that Anthony and I were teaching. We were sharing about the life and death of Stephen, who was martyred in the book of Acts, and this older man wept throughout the whole hour. We had recently found out that his only son, at 21, had been shot and killed a month before. This loving father was so broken that it appeared as if he had only heard the news that day. After class, he sobbed and sobbed about how much it hurt. Anthony and another man put their hands on him and said they didn't have the words, but that they could hug him and support him and pray with the man.

I watched them and felt like God was speaking to me so clearly about this broken-hearted father. I wasn't sure what to do because I never ever pray for men old enough to be my grandpa. I'm a woman and felt it would be more appropriate coming from my husband or the other man who was supporting. As I watched and waited, I could feel the intensity of the desire to speak and the clarity of thoughts rushing in concerning what God wanted him to know at that moment. My heart was pleading for someone else to speak, but the words to speak were in me. I asked Anthony for permission to share what I felt God was impressing and he agreed.

I told the man that I felt so strongly that God wanted him to know that He made him a father, and just because his son was gone didn't mean that he was not going to be a father anymore. All of the fatherly love that he still had would not go to waste. God would give him the strength to father many young and grown men who hadn't known a true father's love. I went on to tell him that God identifies with his brokenness and knows that pain of a father who has lost their only son too. Once I shared this word with him, I prayed for strength for him and told him that every time he gives a father's love to someone on his path, it would be in honor of his son. And that his fathering days would go on well into his old age. I felt so emboldened by the Holy Spirit! I could hear the man praying in the Holy Spirit quietly as I prayed over him and knew that the Holy Spirit was ministering in ways beyond what my words could. The Spirit of the living God was touching this man's heart.

The heaviness seemed to lift and the man continued to talk with us. He explained that he didn't become a Christian until he was 48 and that's when his wife got pregnant. He said everyone at his church had teased him and called him Father Abraham, and they teased his wife and called her Sara. They felt like it made perfect sense to name their son Issac, and that was his beloved son's name—Issac. I was astonished because as he was sharing with what those people said and what he named his son, the man was confirming every word I had prayed over him to be a Father to many just like Father Abraham!

We can't hold back the fragrance of heaven, the comfort of the Holy Spirit in fear. God gives us Himself as a comforter and we get to co-labor with Christ to bring others to the knowledge that God loves them and that *He knows them!* Words are treasures. How wonderful is it that the Holy Spirit trusts us to give treasures to others? When the Holy Spirit gives us words for others, the purpose isn't to bring attention to us as hearers. The purpose of the prophetic is to draw others into the Father's heart. It is for them to know how loved and known they are. Isn't that incredible? That God would let us share treasures of heaven with others? This isn't just for a select few. This is a treasure for every listening heart, everyone who desires to hear and know the Holy Spirit, for everyone who treasures His words.

SPEAKING WHAT YOU HEAR

Speaking the revelation you hear does not have to be super mystical. It can just be a perfectly timed verse that will spark faith in your friend's heart. Speaking revelation is speaking life. It is speaking hope. It is speaking *a better word* on the matter. God's Word is truth and when we consider it, meditate on it, and allow it to come alive to us; it naturally finds its way in our conversations with others.

There are other times, that as you practice walking in an awareness that God is always there and that He is always speaking and He is always mindful of you, that you will hear something specific. It will feel as natural as your own thoughts, but undeniably supernatural too. Like, "I have never thought that before" or "I couldn't know that." For me, it feels like taking a risk. It feels like switching from what I want to do and leaning into what God desires me to do instead. It feels like taking a risk out of my love for God and a love that is greater than my own, for the person listening. It might be a stranger, but the love of God compels me to speak.

Are you a yielded vessel that God can reach out to someone *through* you? Give the Holy Spirit permission to use you. Yield your hearing and yield your speaking. Doesn't that thought give you goosebumps? Yielding can feel risky. That's okay though, we can trust the Holy Spirit and we can know that we can hear His words. His words are treasures that the world desperately needs.

A SEEKING PRAYER
Thank you Holy Spirit that You are with us! Thank you for making God's treasured Word real in us. Thank you for speaking to us and through us to connect hearts to the living God! Holy Spirit, we treasure You. There is nothing better than tending our relationship with You. We posture our heart to listen. We posture our lives to bring glory to You, to Jesus, and to the Father! Thank you for helping us have boldness! We love You and we cherish You!

.

A SOAKING SONG
Holy Spirit (We Love You) by UPPERROOM

CHAPTER FIVE

TREASURE OF A HOUSE

A bout three years ago, when we were seven years into our marriage with three kids and seven years of renting different apartments, homes, and condos, we were finally feeling like we could buy a house. Personally, this particular year felt like it was marked by a redemption that came after enduring a very difficult time filled with physical and spiritual storms. God giving us a house began to make sense to me. Of course, it was time! We didn't give up and quit, and putting down roots would make sense. Situationally, we could also see it was transition time. We began to have difficulty with two of our neighbors, the landlord wanted to raise our rent higher than what we would be paying if we just bought a home of our own, and did I mention that hard year? We had just weathered our first hurricane, experienced a close death, and dealt with severe sleep apnea with our son, Silas.

These hard times had pushed us deeper into our relationship with God, and we were learning to walk in a closeness that we could hear His voice and feel His leading even when everything around us felt shaky. With faith, I began to dream up the perfect house that our family could grow in and we spent the whole summer looking at all the available houses. This exciting time soon became disappointing when we realized that there weren't any houses that held our wish-list in our budget or in the area we wanted to live in. Finally, there was one that seemed like it was going to be, "the one," if I could just accept it's charm and that I needed a small start before we could have a wish-list. No, this house didn't have most of the things on the list. It was located a little too far north and it lacked a needed bedroom, but I began to reason that my boys could continue to share. There was not enough storage because there was only one small hall closet, but it is always good to purge things and become minimalist, right? There also were just a few marks on the inspection that showed the HVAC was not great and some issues in the master bathroom that was smaller than the only other bathroom in the hall.

You may be thinking that it was obviously not our house, but after looking all summer there was one big sign signaling that this was the best that we could do. This small, but cute, house was listed at the very top number of our budget with no wiggle room. We had seen everything available and had to be out of the rental house in weeks. I began to think that maybe I needed to practice thankfulness and recognize that this is the best we can do. Maybe the house was the most that God wanted for us and maybe my list was a little too high—I did put a pool on it after all. Florida is hot, and the home is supposed to be forever, remember? One of my dream items, that I didn't even put on the list because it was just over the top, was for the house to have floor-to-ceiling, built-in bookshelves. I began to think maybe that would be a storage solution! The house didn't have that, but I was sure that with the help of Ikea, I could make it happen. With our hearts full of gratitude, Anthony and I decided to trust that God was providing this little house with the big price tag.

We started the process and two weeks before closing, it was becoming really obvious it was not the right place. The house was so close to being ours that the owner had left a key for us so that we could look around and plan whenever we wanted. On one of those days of planning how this little house would hold our lives; we were sitting in the driveway and I was looking at the tiny garage and began to feel a bit of uneasiness in my heart because I realized that our only vehicle, an SUV, was too big to even fit inside it. The most expensive house we could afford with no storage also had a garage that had no space for our family car. My heart felt gripped with panic and my mind was yelling at me, "What were we thinking, what were we about to do?" I felt scared to back out and scared to move forward. I didn't want to be ungrateful and we needed somewhere to live. I couldn't even articulate my thoughts out loud so I began to pray. I began to pray and ask God that Anthony would just know it wasn't right and confirm what I was feeling. If that didn't happen, I prayed that God would grant me peace to move forward and calm my fears. Thankfully, it wasn't much longer until we both saw the signs that it wasn't the right move and we decided to walk away.

At the time, it felt a little bit like losing. We still didn't have a home we could call ours and we were so close! Days away from holding keys! We felt defeated and as if we wasted everyone's time and money. But deep down, we knew we were making the right decision because there was also the feeling of relief. Just like the good, good Father that He is, God provided us with the perfect rental that showed up on the market that very night because someone had an immediate location change with their job. I remember telling God that I was giving Him that dream of ever owning a house. I told Him that I didn't care if I had to rent for the rest of my life. I told Him that my family was His and I knew that He had always taken good care of us and I knew that He wouldn't stop. My heart was so tired of moving and the uncertainty that comes with renting, but now I felt that trying to buy a house was so disappointing! Resolved not to stay discouraged, I also added to my prayers, *"And by the way, God I never want to buy again unless it has everything on the list!"* And with that, knowing that I was so seen and provided for, I closed the book on that dream.

When I shelved the dream, I thought it was forever. Only, I didn't realize then that God cared about my house dream and more than that, His timing is perfect. He wasn't letting me down but was reserving this kind of answer to a time when I would really need to know that He was for me and He remembers.

Two years later, we found ourselves in a trying time with many relationships going shaky or silent, and not knowing who was with us. Some of these friendships were so close to us and so trusted that they were the very ones who I would've gone to for advice on anything! I looked at these familiar friendships and they weren't to be found, and if they were found, they had letters of accusations in their hands. This time pushed us into a cloud of confusion that led me to seek the One who is not the author of confusion but the Author of Peace! (1 Corinthians 14:33) I couldn't turn to any of my usual places for a "pick me up" of encouragement, not even myself. I found myself asking God about every confusing topic.

One thing about having gone through both valleys and mountains with God is that you know you can talk to Him and you know He will answer you. No matter what, do not shy away from God. In one of my most favorite verses, God says, "Call to me and I will answer you and tell you great and unsearchable things you do not know." (Jeremiah 33:3) The New Living Translation says "remarkable secrets about things to come." God tells us we can come to Him and He says if we come to Him, He will answer us! Ever since I've hidden that verse in the storehouse of my heart, it has been my practice to talk to God about it all! The good, the bad, the ugly! It was in this season that I came to Him saying, *"God, what do you say about forgiveness? God, what do you say about redemption? Is there a point where it runs out? What about forgiving not seven times but seven times seventy? What about a contrite heart? God, what do you say about choosing sides because if I choose a side, let me be on Your side, God, not on the side of any man! If I am guilty of loyalty, let it be to You and You alone!"* And you know what? The Holy Spirit covered me with peace and took me to His treasure words like Romans 8 that opens saying, "Now the case is closed! There remains no accusing voices of condemnation of those who are in Christ." And verses like, "Do you think anyone is going to be able to drive a wedge between us and Christ's love for us? There is no way! Not trouble, not hard times, not hatred, not hunger, not homelessness, not bullying threats, not backstabbing, not even the worst sins listed in Scripture... None of this fazes us because Jesus loves us. I'm absolutely convinced that nothing—nothing living or dead, angelic or demonic, today or tomorrow, high or low, thinkable

> IF YOU DON'T HEAR HIS VOICE, BECAUSE YOUR WORLD IS CONFUSING AND LOUD, OR STRANGELY SILENT AND LONELY, LOOK AROUND AND SEE EVERY SIGN THAT SHOWS HE CARES AND HASN'T FORGOTTEN.

or unthinkable—absolutely nothing can get between us and God's love because of the way that Jesus our Master has embraced us." (Romans 8:35- 37)

No matter how dark a time seems, God still speaks! He has been accused of going silent. There is a common saying that goes, "The teacher doesn't speak in a test." But my Bible tells me all of creation boasts of His name and sings of His provision! If you don't hear His voice, because your world is confusing and loud, or strangely silent and lonely, look around and see every sign that shows He cares and hasn't forgotten. You may be in a test, but your God is walking beside you. The Holy Spirit is handing you words of treasure, gems along the way. God won't let your foot slip. Your protector won't fall asleep on the job. (Psalm 121:3)

It might be a dark place, but in Isaiah 45:3, God spoke to a king who didn't even know Him and was only chasing the wrong things, earthly treasure. God told that king, "I will give you hidden treasures, riches stored in secret places, so that you may know that I am the LORD, the God of Israel, who summons you by name." If

God gives treasures to kings who don't even know Him in order that they *might know* His great Name; how much more will He give the hidden treasures of His word, in the secret places to His children?

In this uncomfortable season, I saw a house that my friend shared on Facebook scroll up on my screen one day. I dismissed it because I was still raw from the last house buying experience and from current events. Last time seemed like the perfect timing, but this time? This time was the worst! I had no mental or emotional space left to even consider starting the process to buy a house. But you know that feeling, where you can't get something out of your head? I didn't even want to look because I knew it was way too much, even though I hadn't seen the price. But I heard a voice within say, *"You said you wouldn't consider anything unless it has everything on your list. This house is actually in your current neighborhood that you really like, and even though you didn't click on it...you can see it has the right number of bedrooms. Are you really not even going to look?"* I may be stubborn, but I try not to be foolish. I decided it wouldn't hurt anything to just look at it. It was an older beach house, for sure, but it did have everything on my list—even a small pool! If that wasn't enough, there was one detail that felt as if this house was intended for me and my family alone—a room that already had built-in, floor-to-ceiling bookshelves!

I called my friend who shared the house because she knew the homeowner, and before the day was over, the homeowner and I were talking on the phone. I should pause to let you know how much of a stretch this was for me. It's hard for me to talk to adults sometimes. You might be laughing and saying, "Brooke, did you know you are an adult?" Yes, I do, but somewhere along the way of ministering to teenagers for the last ten years and becoming a homeschool mom of littles, it's easy to feel like I'm not as "adulty" as everyone else! I find myself defaulting to Anthony and saying, "Will you please call and make this appointment for me?" Or, "Could you just streamline these details for me?" Much to my dismay, it seemed important to God that I learn to use my voice at this time.

At this time, of wanting to be understood by all who turned away from me; *at this time,* of desiring to speak what was firm in my heart, but when I was still shedding the fear of man; in this place, I found myself talking to a complete stranger, the homeowner, who was really more of an angel! She didn't really want to talk to the realtors, but to me, just to me. I was talking about big things like price tags on houses and asking her to consider less. I was negotiating closing matters. Me, the person who felt so unequipped, yet the person who really knew the motives of my heart were pure. Even now, the thought of this process makes me want to hide! But in my heart, I had seen a glimpse that this house was reserved for us! Faith gave me the courage to speak up.

The night before we came to an agreement, this angel lady later told me she had been up that night praying that we would be the homeowners of her home that she had loved for almost twenty years. She didn't know if she would be able to accept the offer, but she felt compelled to look over all the numbers again and again to see if it would work. *She called me* first thing the next morning *to tell me,* "I think there is a miracle concerning you buying the house." She explained that she was able to sell the house for the number we agreed on, but there was no way she could do any better with closing costs. She knew we didn't have any money left for the closing costs because we had put it all into our offer, and she really felt like we were to be the next home owners, so she prayed and crunched numbers. She started laughing a little bit and said, "You're never going to believe this, but I realized that I had made a mathematical error of calculating 8% for realtor fees, where I really only needed 5%. Brooke, the 3% difference is the *exact amount* that you didn't have for the closing costs. The *exact* amount!"

This sweet lady, who I didn't know a week prior, began to tell me that God told her that it was that exact number because she was supposed to help us have this house for our family. I was totally speechless! My heart was racing and my mind was trying to catch up and I heard her say, "Isn't that a miracle? The exact number! Can you believe that? Yes, I accept your offer!" I had no words and could only cry and happily tell her, "Thank you, thank you." There were so many miracles that took place but the loudest one was that the homeowner, a complete stranger, was praying for me! She was praying that God would give me the house of my dreams!

She wasn't the only one speaking. Our realtor had a lot to say too. She said that she never had to do so little communication with a seller or their agent. Trying to understand, she kept asking, "Tell me again how you know the seller?" I had to tell her that I really felt that God wanted to give us this house and the homeowner said she felt like it was supposed to be for us. The realtor didn't quite understand and said, "Yes, umm, I'm sure she does really want to sell her house!" But I just knew it was more than that—God was working on our behalf! The Holy Spirit was speaking also. He gave me a treasured word during this time. Psalm 16:5-6 became the gem of my home! And just like a real jewel I wanted to examine it, in every translation (any emphasis is added)!

> The Lord is my chosen portion and my cup;
> *you hold my lot.*
>
> The lines have fallen for me in pleasant places;
> indeed, <u>I have a beautiful inheritance</u>. (ESV)
>
> You've given me land. You guard all that is mine! (NLT)
>
> My heritage is *beautiful!* (AMP)
>
> My heritage is <u>godly</u>! (KJV)
>
> Your path leads to pleasant places! (TPT)
>
> *You've set me up with a house and a yard!* (MSG)

He gave me other Word treasures, "So I gave you a land on which you did not toil and cities you did not build; and you live in them and eat from vineyards and olive groves that you did not plant." (Joshua 24:13) He reminded me this wasn't my doing, my toiling or my building, but it was a gift from my Father. He made a way, and no man or opinion or timing could stand in His way. Who could alter His plans? I had a long, long list of miracles concerning this house that only could be credited back to God! This treasure of a house wasn't one that I was seeking out or diligently looking for. It was a dream that I had put on a shelf while saying, *"God, even if You never do it, I'm okay with that. I have all I want anyways."* The treasure of my house reminds me that God delights in giving good gifts to his children. (Matthew 7:11)

> WHEN YOU USE YOUR VOICE, YOU PUT FAITH AND ACTION TO THE TREASURE YOU HAVE RECEIVED.

It's the treasure of knowing some things can only come about if I use my voice. When you use your voice, you put faith and action to the treasure you have received. Speaking, taking action, in faith shows the value of the words you've let grow in your heart. It's like the Maverick City song that says, "If you said it we believe it! You're a man of your word!"

I don't know if I would even be writing this now, if I hadn't heard His word on this matter. Maybe, I would still be renting our old house. I, definitely, don't think I would be brave enough to share my heart. His words give us courage! That's why His words are treasures! One word of God lets you hold on and believe for other promises not yet fulfilled. You can confidently contend for other victories, even now, because you can rely on the past times He spoke and came through for you! You will begin to say,

"God spoke to me on that,
God did this for me then,
God calmed my heart then,
and I *know* He will speak again!"

It is against His very character to change—He is steadfast and trustworthy. You will feel like the disciples who said, *"Did our hearts not burn within us while he talked to us and opened up the scriptures?"* (Luke 24:32) You will not be simply looking at the past words, but it causes your heart to burn within and puts hope in you that even tomorrow, my God has treasured words for me!

MORE THAN YOUR WILDEST DREAMS

God can do anything He wants to, in any way that He sees fit. It doesn't matter if it makes sense to us. It doesn't matter if it seems naturally possible or even if it makes sense to everyone. It's a crazy thought that though He can do anything, He desires to do the miraculous with us and through us. We know that it is miraculous because we know our own limitations, our insecurities, and that these things we could never ever do on our own.

We've got a good Father who backs us. Let that free you up today! You don't have to be good enough, confident enough, and it doesn't matter for a minute what other people think or say. There is one Voice above all others, and that Voice says, *"You are Mine and Dad's got you. Go ahead and step out."* Did you know the fact that you don't feel capable shows humility? It's brave to know that you are taking action beyond what you know you can do and it is faith knowing that He's got you. It's only when we don't act because we feel incapable that we remain stuck.

What is the wildest thing you desire? Not carnal desires, but the purest, wildest desire? Ask Him! Surrender it. Bury that thing and keep your eyes on Him, the totality of all you desire. The way of miracles is first death, then resurrection. If you've hidden that desire in Him and are chasing after Him, the things He has for you, your true desires, will come across your radar...pay attention! It might be time to take action.

"God can do anything, you know—far more than you could ever imagine or guess or request in your wildest dreams! He does it not by pushing us around but by working within us, his Spirit deeply and gently within us."
(Ephesians 3:20 MSG)

A SEEKING PRAYER
God, thank you that I can look back and see the miracle of a house! The miracle of You making a way, and using my voice to make that way! Let us look at Your past goodness and kindness and feel courage to bravely speak and act. We know that we have all of heaven backing us when we are aligned with Your will. We know that if we are not headed in the right direction that You are kind and will help us find a better way. Today, we ponder in our hearts the treasures we know only You could've provided. We love You!

A SOAKING SONG
Man of Your Word by Maverick City Music Group

CHAPTER SIX

WHEN DISSATISFIED TURNS TO DESPERATION

S o many of us are relationally driven. We seek to know how to find our tribe or our circle. We long for the support of others that say we understand you and we are here for you. We also feel that when we find "our people" we can respond and give better because we understand what they need. We will spend countless hours reading or listening to podcasts or speaking to a good friend on how to be better.

Better at everything—
more attentive,
more loving,
stronger,
less distracted,
less triggery,
less ungrateful,
and on and on the list goes.

A better spouse, parent, child, teacher, friend or whatever relational role that most consumes our thoughts at the moment.

This is not a terrible thing. It comes from a very good place. If it is not out of some place of despair or self-loathing, it most likely is out of a place of love and giving. We want to relate the best parts of us to those around us and those that we love the most. It comes from a place of wanting to take the worst parts of us and smooth them out and sweeten them up to be able to make a better connection to those in our spheres.

Sometimes, our best intentions can turn it into an ugly thing or an obsession. We know this isn't right and that's not what I'm talking about. There are countless "pick yourself up," be brave, and celebrate your efforts messages out there; but in this chapter, I want to tell you how, as a relationally driven lover of people, (especially *my* people—my husband, my children, my friends), there was a season that I was neglecting the most important driving relationship of all—my relationship with God.

I must stop right here to say loudly that at this time I *loved* God. I had given my life to Him many, many years prior and I had put every dream and hope into living *for* Him. I had been in full-time ministry for eleven years, but somewhere along the way, between marriage and adding children and life's countless leaking moments, I had begun to lose a deep, *current* connection to my relationship with God. And a current, intimate connection in this relationship, that is above all other relationships, creates an order that can't be achieved any other way.

As I drifted, I found myself in a place where walls were closing in around me. The walls were made up of all things that I did not like and that I did not ask for. They came about quickly and suddenly and my spirit felt crushed. It was 2016, the year we lost big; the year my inner circle moved to different states, all very far away—quickly they left, one by one. As that last close friend departed, my family weathered our first hurricane. Now in retrospect, the hurricane was a symbol of the strengthening of the strongest spiritual storm that personally touched my home, my husband, my children, and my heart. Immediately, after the relief of the hurricane passing, came the first time that I had experienced death and loss so closely. My house was intact, but *my home* felt devastated. For the first time, I had to have conversations about the death of a loved one with my five-year-old, Silas. That same year, Silas was battling sleep apnea that required many sleep studies, sleeping with a cpap for four months, and badly needing surgery that kept getting delayed. It was a year of anxiety and tension. The stop-you-in-your-tracks-and-grab-your-heart kind. It was the year of holding my husband's hand silently, in solidarity, because neither of us could express the deep feelings of loss and hurt that had touched our house.

Oh, but the year that intended to make me feel so weak; actually gave me one of the greatest gifts. In such a hard place of trial, I found myself moving away from apathy and hurriedness to a place of inextinguishable hunger for God's Word like never before. It hadn't always been that way. There were always good excuses to keep me in shallow reading or reading out of duty of any prepared plan that sounded like something that I would like. The love of God was always there, but the desire to know Him at a greater level was dampened by my attitude of I KNOW God and I feel us "doing life together" and I'm trying to live well. But God unlocked something in me during this season of loss. In this place of barely being able to come up for air, I felt the deep desire to KNOW God more *right now.*

> GOD INSTILLED IN ME THE DEEPEST DESIRE TO MOVE FROM SERVANT OF GOD OF THE COSMOS TO DAUGHTER OF A LOVING GOD THAT SAYS I CAN CRAWL UP INTO HIS LAP.

I KNEW God, I did, but I needed to HEAR HIM NOW.
And I needed to know He HEARD ME too.
Deeper. Not shallow, but DEEP!

In this place of discomfort, God instilled in me the deepest desire to move from servant of God of the cosmos to daughter of a loving God that says I can crawl up into His lap. Many of us know that we are children of God, but are content with merely living as servants. Faithful one, there is more than "quick and easy" and check-the-box living. Unwavering one, there's more depths to see, hear, experience, and know! He speaks now and beyond devotionals in another author's pen or worship from another believer's praise. Curious and New one, He speaks to those He is in a relationship with and connected to. You could gaze at Him forever and not grow tired. He is Maker. He is Husband. He is Father. He is the Great Defender, the Strong Tower. He is our All in All!

In this time and place of many trials, I couldn't lean only on the comfort of what I knew, or rely on how I felt. That wasn't enough. I needed the God who knew me and saw me, to speak priceless words to me personally. I needed to hear the voice behind me telling me, *"This is the way and walk in it,"* and whether to turn to the right or the left (Isaiah 30:12). It wasn't enough to just know that there was a voice and He was there, I needed to know what He was saying now. I needed to return to Him and seek Him. And when I did, I found Him and the rich reward of knowing Him.

{ YOU CAN BE IN A SEA OF CONFUSION AND HE WILL CALM THE WATERS SO THAT YOU CAN HEAR AND SEE HIM AND KNOW THAT YOU ARE KNOWN BY HIM. }

He keeps good on His promises and He said, *"Seek and you will find."* (Matthew 7:7) Through heartache, trials, and a strong distaste of urgency, I found myself safe in the strong grasp of the Father. I felt His mighty Hand uphold me. I felt it bottle up tears and prayers, even the ones that were but a whisper. I felt those broken places spill out depths when I thought I was at the end of me. In the midst of loss and confusion, there is a loving Father to behold. We like to quote that God is not the God of confusion and that's correct, but sometimes we are sitting right there in confusion. God is not troubled by that. You can be in a sea of confusion and He will calm the waters so that you can hear and see Him and know that you are known by Him.

"Your steps formed a highway through the seas with footprints on a pathway no one even knew was there. You led your people forward by your loving hand."
(Psalm 77:19-20a TPT)

THERE IS MORE

For some, we may have many years of church going or studying the Bible and books. Maybe you are like me, and can say how long you've been a believer, or how much you do, in fact, love God. Others might be so brand new and just starting to dip their feet in the oceans of His love, that you've only begun a relationship with God and aren't really sure how to grow. The question for everyone is the same and the treasure is found in the answer. Is the desire to know God [still] the strongest desire that I have?

To know God the most—above all the other roles you have—do you have an obsession and longing to know God more, to store His words in the chambers of your heart like treasure? Maybe you have gotten to a place in your journey where you say, "Oh, I know God. Yes, I love Him! I'm a believer and I'm a Christian," and you can talk about what He has done for you, but could it be that knowing Him already is actually keeping you from knowing Him more? Dare I say, you know Him a little? Because there is always more and more to know! Maybe knowing Him more doesn't feel like the most pressing thing because right now you need to know how to stop yelling, or how to enjoy your current season or how to deal with a really big issue of life.

The issues of life can weigh down even the strongest. You may feel like if it was just one thing that you could handle it. But not this...this is too much. Sometimes it feels as if you don't even have the ability to verbalize what you're going through because everything looks okay on the outside. My friend, if you're having trouble seeing through heartache and uncertainty, or busyness, there is more to behold.

Life gets loud. Our good intentions are loud. The noise can drown out our desire to be in a present, deep relationship with God. Relationship with God is so much more than what we do. It is more than a love of worship music. It is more than prioritizing the things God likes, or simply being a good person. There is a relational God that we can be connected to. He will deepen and set right every other relationship we have. God loves you so much that He will never let anything slip that is good for you or that you care deeply about! A relational God who sees, hears, *speaks,* and knows you fully. And what's even better, He's a God that can be known!

There is a somewhat dangerous, comfortable attitude that can prevent us from knowing Him more. A comfort that unconsciously says, *"This relationship is here and it is good so I better focus on these things that need more attention."* It's this familiarity and staleness that causes the world to see the lives of many Christians and think that their lives and issues are just the same as mine, but that Christians also have the chores of religion. They must be wondering what's the point of it all? Maybe if you're honest, you have felt like that too. As you try to examine your own relationship with God, you will begin to realize that so much of relationship can't be told, and isn't found in lists or behaviors; but has to be experienced. If you feel stagnant, I challenge you that there is more of God that you can apprehend—

More knowledge,
More experience,
More satisfaction,
More wholeness,
More to behold!

God will make every other relationship fall into place and meet every need. Release your cares into His care. Psalm 16 says, "The boundary lines will fall in pleasant places." If He is limitless, then you haven't maxed out on closeness. There is more! Are you desperate?

A SEEKING PRAYER

Holy Spirit, help us to hear. We thank you for times that cause our desperation to grow and we ask forgiveness for times that we have been so very busy and distracted from the most important thing—dwelling with You! No matter what type of season we are in today, we ask You to fill every bit of our heart with You. We lean into You, we want to hear what You have to say. It is the most important thing and we need it to get through each day! If we find ourselves in a hard season, we lean into the fact that we can trust You today. If it's not good yet, You're not done. Surely Your goodness will surround those who love You! We can trust You and we know that You are with us and that You have a present word that You will speak to us even now.

A SOAKING SONG
Take Me Deeper by Far Flung Tin Can

CHAPTER SEVEN

SETTLE

Anthony surprised me with my first international trip to Ireland for our tenth wedding anniversary. We found out we were pregnant with our first son, Silas, on our one year wedding anniversary; and not long after came Ezra and Ruby. This bucket list trip was a big deal for the obvious reasons, but also we had never been away from our kids for this long. A little bit nervous and very excited, I was awake late at night trying to get comfortable in my seat on the airplane.

We were flying at night and were halfway to our destination. I had my sleep mask fixed into position. My music was not working out and I didn't like the selection they provided; so I opted to simply hear all the cabin bustle around me. This created the most shallow sleep so I began to pray for greater revelation in the situations that had been surrounding us. I began to pray things like Gideon must have, *"There's an army coming and when we don't know what to do we keep our eyes on You!"* I tossed and turned knowing that physically, I was going to be tired tomorrow, but spiritually I was going to be built up from allowing my body to stay in that shallow state of rest while my spirit was deep in prayer, as deep in prayer that you could be and still hear the person next to you order chicken and red wine, deep in heart but completely aware of your present surroundings.

> INSTEAD OF SEEING THEN PRAYING, BUT PRAYING AND ASKING, "HOLY SPIRIT, WHAT IS IT YOU SEE? SHOW ME WHAT TO SEE HERE."

The more I grow, the more convinced I am, that this is the place the Holy Spirit is calling me to dwell; very in touch with my present reality, but my eyes deeply closed because my spirit is conversing with Abba on the matter. A constant, *"This is what is before me, Holy Spirit, what do You say? My eyes are on You because I know that You are going to move. It's not that I think if I look away I might miss it, but I want to behold Your mighty move because You have my full attention."* There's a place where we can rest with our full attention focused on God, but still be very aware of everything going on around us. Sometimes what we hear will bombard and interrupt our thoughts and prayers, and we have to will our flesh to remain where our spirit wants to be. Isn't that it? That's where I found myself in that season. I'm wondering, even now after the surroundings have changed, if I'm ever supposed to leave that state. I'm beginning to think not. I'm beginning to think that it is more important to be spirit-led than to be led by what's before me. Oh, if we can reverse how we see! Instead of seeing then praying, but praying and asking, *"Holy Spirit, what is it You see? Show me what to see here."*

Our flight was relatively smooth, but we hit a patch of turbulence that lasted for a while. The flight attendants were assisting different passengers and tending to their needs. Previously, they were cleaning, preparing, and working on things that they knew needed to happen even if the others on the plane weren't aware. The seat belt sign chimed and everyone knew that the rough air we had been experiencing needed to be acknowledged for their own safety. The flight attendants rushed as they reminded the passengers the light was on and to keep buckled. A few more minutes went by, then the pilot came on the speaker and said, "Flight attendants, please secure yourself in the jump chairs."

While praying, I caught myself turning those words over and over in my head. "Please secure yourselves in your jump chairs." The pilot just came over the speaker and gave them a clear direction on what they needed to do. It didn't matter if others were still asking them for things or even if they were used to flying over rough air. Jump chairs. Not exactly the most encouraging words to hear when you're on a plane over the middle of the Atlantic Ocean and traveling through rough air. *Are we jumping somewhere? Do I need to get one of those?* The Holy Spirit then illuminated to me that in that place—the jump chair—the pilot's attendants were secure, prepared for any impact. These chairs were specifically prepared for them. There they could rehearse all the safety procedures without the distractions of questions or other flight duties. All of the people and all of the things could wait because for their good, they needed to be seated in a chair that was designated for them for such a time as this.

> YOUR GOOD CAPTAIN WANTS TO TAKE YOU OUT OF AN INSECURE SPOT AND PLACE YOU IN A SEAT OF SECURITY!

In the jump chair, they could brace themselves for impact, not sudden death impact, or "we are going to crash impact," but they could brace themselves for the bumps and blows that might jump and jar them if they were anywhere else besides a secure, settled location. They would still feel this segment of rough air on our otherwise smooth flight, but with the security of being in a place made to handle it. What a good Captain! He told them exactly what they needed to do. Not in so many words or with an explanation. Nor did he ask their opinion. I can only imagine that he saw what we were entering into from a different perspective than those of us in the cabin. He knew that it was for their good to be in a fixed position that was prepared ahead of time for them. It was more important to be settled and all the things and people could wait.

Your Father is just like that good Captain and wants to make you secure—physically, emotionally, and spiritually. Secure means fixed, protected—not loose, not threatened, safe, stable, free from fear! Your good Captain wants to take you out of an insecure spot and place you in a seat of security!

"But may the God of all grace, who called us to His eternal glory by
Christ Jesus, after you have suffered a while, perfect, establish,
strengthen, and settle you."
(1 Peter 5:10 NKJV)

The God who knows and sees, pricked my heart and said, *"It's just like that isn't it? Oh, when it's rough if you only get in the jump chair and fasten yourself securely. I will settle you. You don't have to think about the storm, dwell on the storm, or embrace for sudden death! You just need to rehearse in your mind, everything you already know to be true, and prepare your heart to stay in a position of peace. In the chair designated for you, you can speak the Word, you can pray, and you can rest assured that the good Captain will tell you only what you need to know. Where do you think the safest spot is? Just because you are trained, and you have been through other storms, and you still have people turning on their call lights asking you for so many things, that doesn't give you license to ignore the Captain. You get in that jump chair so that you can be settled and your heart filled with courage. Rest there, be settled."*

Wouldn't it be crazy if the flight attendant decided to keep pouring coffee in the turbulence? It would not be very safe for her or for the person who wanted it! How crazy would it be if she started knocking on the pilot's cabin and said, "Umm are you sure? It seems like it is about to pass and I've been through similar storms so I think I can handle this. It's just that I am really busy. I know you know best but if you would just let me quickly get a few more things done, I would really feel much better about resting. Let me check off a couple more things on my list, then I'll rest, no problem!"

No way would that ever happen! But isn't that what we do sometimes when our hearts hear a command that cramps our plans? Our pilot is gentle, and doesn't need to repeat Himself when He's sure we got the message. The issue isn't with the pilot. Sometimes it's us that have trouble sitting in that prepared place of safety and rest. Settled. Oh, how good it is to know that He will settle us!

How precious is the Holy Spirit to speak to our hearts the exact words of life we need to hear? As soon as I fished out my laptop to begin pouring out these words, everything began to feel smooth again. While I was writing, I watched the light wake up over all the clouds and it literally looked like heaven surrounded. Where did the storm go? Just one word of peace from the Holy Spirit and the surrounding conditions changed.

"Forever, O Lord, Your word is settled in heaven."
(Psalm 119:89 NKJV)

His Word is settled! His treasured words of promise are for you! His Word, the Bible, which is yours to stand on. It's settled! "What then shall we say to these things? If God is for us, who can be against us? He who did not spare his own Son but gave him up for us all, how will he not also with him graciously give us all things?" (Romans 8:31-32) What more can we say, Paul says! If God is for us, if He didn't even spare his own Son while we were still undeserving sinners, do you really think He is going to withhold from you? Paul is basically saying, "Hey, trust God! Get in the jump chair, sit down and rehearse the truth! Who can be against you?"

PHYSICALLY SHALLOW, SPIRITUALLY DEEP

God is so faithful to speak. He is always speaking, but we have to tune our hearts to listen. Maybe it's that physically shallow, but spiritually deep place we need to find ourselves in more frequently to experience hearing the Divine greater. The place where you are still totally aware of every detail surrounding you, but your spirit is saying, *"I don't care about any of that, I'm conversing with You, my relational God, because You know exactly where I am physically and spiritually and You are holding it all together and for my good."* Even in rough patches, you can settle yourself in a secured position at His spoken directions. You can know it won't be long until you are soaring smoothly through buttery clouds while the world wakes. There are greater depths to behold and no matter your situation, you can have the treasure of being settled at His Word.

And it's not just turbulent times, we can turn our gaze to Him in all things! If something incredible happens, *"God, did You see that? That was so amazing, that was You, wasn't it? I praise You!"* Or it can be in the ordinary. We are the sons and daughters of God and we can know that He is with us in every situation. God is always there and He is relational to us in His care for us and He is relational, as in proximity to us. It is we who need to move our gaze to where He is. For His service. For His delight. For a greater communion. We can't be content to put all these things of God in boxes where one might label it too legalistic and another too mystic.

The one who has seen the God who knows and sees has moved on from labeling any of this like a legal contract and knows it is a bond of love. The one who has seen the God who knows and sees knows there's so much more to behold, to be heard, to be known. They are okay with some things taking them by surprise because they know they can't possibly know it all and they are okay with that. In turbulence, He may be saying, *"Go to the jump chair, be settled at my Word."* In the good times, He may be saying, *"You're my joy! I'm singing over you!"* In times of questioning, He is saying, *"I am right here, my child."* He is always speaking, and if you're like me, you're not always listening. Oh how grateful we can be for those turbulent times! Though we don't like them, they teach us that He is always, always there and most importantly, that He always holds us safely. We make it through every time. Look around, strong one, look how much you've survived! You've lived to sing His praises!

"God is in the midst of her, she shall not be moved;
God shall help her, just at the break of dawn."
(Psalm 46:5 NKJV)

No matter what you are going through, rough air or smooth sailing, God is with you! Listen to His voice. He is most certainly going to settle you and keep you in a firm place.

A SEEKING PRAYER

God, thank you! Thank you for being so close to us. Thank you that we can be so deep in discussion with You even though presently it seems like there are a bunch of things going on around us. This dialogue with You is the most important place for our minds to dwell! It is the place where You build our spirits up strong! We can teach our body to wait and to move past what it sees and hears and listen for You. God, You're faithful! You are the God who sees and knows and is aware. Your Word, settles us! When we read it, You presently speak to our hearts. Thank you for knowing exactly what we need on this very day.

A SOAKING SONG

Once we arrived at our destination, I told Anthony to read over this chapter about what I felt that God was speaking to me. After He read it, we both remembered a new album released while we were traveling that we wanted to listen to and so we started the download. Anthony started to laugh and said to look at the name of the first song. It was named *Settle.* Coincidence? No, not for one actively seeking to hear their God, their personal God, who knows them inside and out.

Settle by The Family

THERE IS NO LACK

"O [reverently] fear the Lord, you His saints (believers, holy ones);
For to those who fear Him there is no want...But they who seek the
Lord will not lack any good thing."
(Psalm 34:9 – 10b)

I
n Him, there is no lack. In Him, you have no lack. There are misconceptions that if you speak of having no lack that you are speaking out of a prosperity gospel mentality. The "name it and claim it" type of prayers—an ideology that is supposed to promote superiority and seems to fill your arms with all things and your bellies to full. An idea that says since you believe in God and you believe and know truth, then you can simply declare things as yours. This kind of thinking always makes me think of a genie who will grant you a few good wishes, but there's not any responsibility or a connection of relationship. It's you know the One who gives and you know the formula of prayer; but the formula doesn't always work. The formula being—ask God, then say, *"Oh please this, oh please that...if you do, I promise I'll..."*

Perhaps, this is why some people don't pray. They think it doesn't really matter because they can't figure out the formula. They promised that for the rest of their life, they would do this and that, if this one thing came to pass, but it didn't, so it must all be happenstance. My friend, you need to know the formula doesn't always work because there is no formula. When we approach prayer like a means to an end we are actually offering up unauthorized prayers. Unauthorized because they are not according to God's will or supported by a consecrated heart. Sometimes, we may get lucky or in God's grace He will answer us in our childishness, but prayer is not a formula that we can memorize.

There is the other polarizing idea that because we are to take part in Christ's suffering that we have to keep our head low and our skin tough because there is one thing you can count on—hard times. The world is going to hell in a handbasket and a Judicial God is going to shoot lightning bolts down. Justifiably, too. Surely, He is so preoccupied passing judgement on evil that He wouldn't even notice us. We are good with the judge because we feel to some degree that we are better than others. We at least try. There's a whole bunch of judgement that needs to be handed out; so our hard times are just a sign that we are getting off easy compared to others. Which is true? Both of these ideas seem so far from each other, both seem to be missing it so big. Missing what? Connection to His heart for us, connection to what the scriptures say about who He is...remember God told Moses His very name in Exodus 34! His name tells us His ways!

Merciful
    Gracious
        Slow to Anger
            Abiding in Steadfast Love
                Abounding in Lovingkindness

Abiding in Him, you will not lack any good thing. Apart from Him, there is no good thing. He is all that is good. Good isn't a weak word that is found in the middle of bad and best. Good is the word that God used when He looked at His creation! When He created an expanse and called it heaven and created land with rolling hills and mountain ranges and the sea, He called His creation, the actualization of His spoken Word, *good*. When Moses, a friend of God, asked to see His face, what did He do? God told Moses His name, His characteristics, and allowed His *goodness* to pass before him. Friend of God, you can expect good things to follow you as you follow Him. This isn't pie in the sky, but when you are around Goodness, Himself, you will be surrounded by good!

Sometimes though, we have to look hard to see the good. It doesn't mean that He is far away or that we are far away. It's just that in our world, where two kingdoms are constantly rivaling for our attention, we are at best, looking through that foggy mirror that Corinthians 13 tells us about. We know in part, and we see in part. Feet on Earth, eyes fixed towards the Heavens. If our gaze drops, we can easily see those giants tangible right before us. Bills, bad reports, things that we thought we were through, but there they are.

There have been many times I remember payday approaching, and trusting God that there would be no lack and that we wouldn't be begging for bread. There was one time where before the month had even started finances were tight. I remember payday felt far away (at that time we were paid once a month and really had to stretch it), and we had less than usual and knew that the coming month had an additional unexpected bill that would take all the extra...and there wasn't a whole lot of extra to begin with! In one of my times of prayer, I looked at the size of the bill and counted how many calendar days until the next time our account would see money... and this was all before the initial pay day had even happened! I was *pre-worrying, pray-worrying* before I even needed to.

I felt so frustrated. Not so much at God, but really at myself because I knew that He had always provided. I knew that I had experienced miracles where the numbers did not make sense, yet we had made it. I didn't have just a head knowledge of what the Word says about provision; I had experiential knowledge that there is no lack when we put it all in His hands! So why, oh why, did I see the extra bills, the amount coming in, only once, and think of what else might show up? Why was it in my nature to think that I needed to pray for the best, but prepare for the worst? I felt my spirit rise up within me and say, *"No! Not this time."* I told God that I wasn't going to do that for the next 28 days because it didn't put my heart in the right place; it didn't place Him in the highest place. Instead, I was going to expect good and unexpected things. It is in His character to show goodness and kindness, and unfortunately, it's in mine to be worrying or grumbling and miss it all together!

I really do want to praise Him. I love and desire God, but my mind will fixate on the preparation and planning that I must do to steward well.

> ANYONE CAN HELP ME TROUBLESHOOT MY FINANCES OR COME UP WITH A GOOD SCHEDULE FOR MY WEEK, BUT WHO, EXCEPT ME, CAN HOLD ON TO MY PEACE, DESPITE ANY SITUATION I FACE?

That sounds like a good Christian principle, to steward well. And it is, but maybe we know we are to steward in our heads, but in our practice we are doing it wrong. To steward means to manage what you have. We can look at stewarding as we must be thinking about and planning for every possible situation we may face and that is being a good steward of our things and our life. But to me, that sounds a lot like trying to be in control. And when we have trouble maintaining control, it turns into worry.

Maybe, we can look at stewarding a different way if we place the emphasis not on our worldly things but instead on, *"How do I take care of the treasures that God has given me? How can I tend to my peace? How can I offer up everything to God for Him and for His use and grow my faith?"* Anyone can help me troubleshoot my finances or come up with a good schedule for my week, but who, except me, can hold on to my peace, despite any situation I face? Who else can take the measure of faith that I have and see that it grows? Worrying and good planning will never take care of these treasures!

In that super tight month, I decided I was going to take note of each blessing... with the only stipulations being that it had to be unexpected and it had to be a financial gain (something I couldn't have had if I didn't spend money). Every good thing comes from Him, so I knew that each unexpected blessing was His love. And my heart wanted to take notice. I wanted to say, *"God I know You take care of me each and every time that things get tight or a little difficult. Every single time You do, You're so faithful! I don't want to let any bit of Your loving kindness be too small for me to see or too under appreciated. I often don't even notice until the end of the month with a big sigh like, 'Oh God we made it! Thank you!' But I don't want to wait until You come through to say thank you. If You're painting a miracle out of this month, I want to watch every brush stroke! I want to notice and say, 'God I see You! I am known and seen and I know and see You too!'"*

And in the tightest month of the whole year, there were more unexpected little (and big) daily things than ever before—like spending $3 when I expected to spend $40; pulling into a full parking meter; a lady graciously giving our family eggs all month for the first time. Things we could have never afforded on a good month like free tickets for Silas, my seven-year-old, and his dad to go to a theme park. Even something that I really needed, like the homeschool curriculum, was given as a gift; a weekend of meals because our family was in town and loved on us; a $100 bill placed in my husband's hand, and so many other things were provided in the tightest month of all.

Showers and showers of unexpected good things! You might think, oh this seems a little bit silly, childish even, to be looking so hard for good things. In fact, these things aren't a big deal and you're reaching. If you told me this, I would have to simply smile at you as if I'd discovered the biggest secret and tell you that you are right! It is childish! And even if it seems as if I was delusional on a treasure hunt for things that I did not earn or deserve; I would have to tell you, "Yes, that was exactly how it was!" Isn't that kind of the point? Didn't Jesus tell us that we are to become like children to inherit the kingdom of God? Like a child, expect the good, don't prepare for the worst and take notice! Abba, our Father, is providing for you not in a lump sum kind of way, but in daily, tender care. His mercies are new every morning! His care isn't rigid and only just what we need or what we deserve. His care brings us good and lacks nothing.

"If you then, though you are evil, know how to give good gifts to your children, how much more will your Father in heaven give the Holy Spirit to those who ask him!"
(Luke 11:13)

My favorite unexpected good thing happened when my husband and Ezra, who at the time was only four, went to the car wash. While waiting in the empty waiting room that had a gumball machine, my little guy, a true sugar bug, noticed and really wanted a gumball. This time, he wasn't throwing a tantrum, just really hoping with a childlike longing for one of those shiny green or red balls to roll down the twisty lane of the machine and into his hand. Anthony told him, "Sorry buddy, I don't have any quarters." They sat waiting alone watching the cars go through the wash when all of the sudden, Ezra shrieked excitedly. He pointed and said, "DAD! Look!" and there on the side of an end table sat not one, but two quarters. One would have been nice. But two? Doesn't God sometimes show off a little bit to us? Both of those guys got a big, juicy gumball!

God cares about four-year-olds who wish for a gumball, and He even cares for dads who are 24 days into a tight month and have said, "No, sorry," more frequently than usual. He even cares enough to provide not one, but two quarters. He doesn't care that gumballs are silly and their flavor doesn't last. He knows that what will last is the impression that His goodness makes on your heart. He cares about the littlest and most insignificant desires of your heart when you've placed all your desire on having Him in the highest place of your heart. How do I know? Because He shows us his character when we are looking at Him.

ANXIETY TO ANTICIPATION

God wants to change our anxious thought patterns to anticipation. Anxiety is feeling worried or uncertain about an outcome. It is being nervous about uncertainty and not even knowing why you feel that way. At the heart of the word, anxiety means distressed and antsy. The root word in Latin means to choke. But anticipation is a feeling of SURENESS. Anticipation says

{ ANTICIPATION IS A FEELING OF SURENESS }

this will happen, I expect this to happen, I predict it will go this way! Sometimes our anticipation can be so great that we even have to apologize because it can cause us to act before we know based on how sure our expectation is.

Your God, who is so aware of all things concerning you, wants to change your anxiety to anticipation. He wants you to feel so sure about what He thinks of you and how He acts on your behalf; that you are living in a place of anticipation, sureness, and expectation! Just like children do! So where do you find yourself today? Sitting in plenty and singing praises? Or maybe you are pray-worrying and you are actually sitting in plenty, but you don't see it yet because your eyes need to be fixed on the Lord. Fear...reverently worship...He is faithful. A. W. Tozer said, "If He is unchanging, it follows that He could not be unfaithful, since that would require Him to change." You can count on Him!

A SEEKING PRAYER

Father, open our eyes to Your goodness to us today! Not that we think You are a genie in the sky, but God we know that You care. You are our treasure; in You we have no lack, because You are all that is of worth! The other stuff is just your kindness to us! If today brings suffering, and it may, we still have You, and we are not alone! If today is one of the good ones, we know it's from You, we say, "Thank you!"

A SOAKING SONG

I'll Give Thanks by Housefires

CHAPTER NINE

WATER IN A WILDERNESS AND IN A STADIUM

The wilderness. It's crazy, right? It's broad, not touched by many, and definitely not touched enough to make a mark on it's vast expanse. It's untamed and full of wildlife just thriving in all its undomesticated goodness! For some, it can spark the call of adventure to go off the grid and get lost. For others, like myself, the most opposite of outdoorsy, the sheer magnitude of the wilderness and lack of control over the environment is enough to make one not even consider it. When driving on our long road trips, I'll catch myself gazing out the window just thinking about how crazy it would be if we had to travel that untrodden path like the pioneers did, instead of the road we are on. I imagine it would have been such a feat that once the pioneers got to their destination, they would never want to go back to where they came from! They had to have been so sure and full of courage!

If you're like me then you are so thankful for the modern world and it's modes of transportation! Sometimes when we fly to our destination and we are close to our landing, my children want to look out the window and see all the trees that look like broccoli and pretend to eat them! From the aerial view, the wilderness is still amazing! It's huge and no matter how much we cultivate around it, could you ever count all the trees? It would take so long to take notice of them all—from the mature ones, to the ones just sprouting up! The wilderness that is wild and alive and full of potential held a lot of significance to the people who found themselves trudging through wilderness experiences in the Bible.

In Genesis 16, Abraham and Sara's servant, Hagar, is caught between them. Sara was growing tired of waiting on God's promise and got the idea to help God out by giving Hagar to Abraham so that she might carry his promise. This backfired when Hagar happily conceived and was a little less than gracious to Sara. Actually, Genesis says that she was arrogant and disrespectful. It would truly be cruel to make someone who wanted a baby so badly feel insignificant on purpose, but that's how the Amplified version words it. Sara grew jealous and returned fire for fire, with hatred and humiliation as her weapons, and Hagar fled from her. Probably running for her life or just out of despair, Hagar found herself in the wilderness with no one and no direction. I love what Genesis 16:7 says, "But the Angel of the Lord found her by a spring of water."

> And He said, "Hagar, Sarai's maid, where did you come from and where are you going?" And she said, "I am running away from my mistress Sarai." The Angel of the Lord said to her, "Go back

to your mistress, and submit humbly to her authority." Then the Angel of the Lord said to her, "I will greatly multiply your descendants so that they will be too many to count." The Angel of the Lord continued, "Behold, you are with child, and you will bear a son; and you shall name him Ishmael (God hears), because the Lord has heard and paid attention to your persecution (suffering). Then she called the name of the Lord who spoke to her, *"You are God Who Sees;"* for she said, "Have I not even here [in the wilderness] remained alive after seeing Him [*who sees me with understanding and compassion*]?" (Genesis 16:8-13 AMP)

How much grace and redemption is in this encounter? Hagar, I can relate to, because sometimes the very reason that I am lost in a wilderness is the result of my own mistakes. My own pride or poor choices have a long history of leaving me so stuck without a lot of options! My pride will say, *"You deserve this so don't feel bad. You've earned it, it's okay to enjoy the feelings of success."* But oh pride, how you leave us quickly the moment things get difficult. Suddenly, oh no, it's me who got me here and now what am I going to do? Poor choices made by poor thought patterns will leave us lost every time.

Thank you Jesus, for teaching us of Abba who seeks out the lost! The Old Testament accounts like Genesis 16 testifies to this too! It isn't just a new God that goes after the lost to bring them direction and hope. No! That is in the very character of Yahweh! Hagar, who was arrogant and disrespectful, and getting what she probably deserved was found by an angel of the Lord. He didn't chastise her and tell her that she really screwed up. He didn't tell her that she should've behaved more lovely. No, He gave her direction and promise. He told her that God hears and that he pays attention to her suffering! This wasn't an empty word or merely a positive thought. When the *rhema,* spoken word of God, comes to you, it is a revival to your faith. It illuminates your situation through the lens of *God knows me.* Hagar, who didn't previously know she could call out to God in distress, responded to the Lord and said, "You are the God who sees." The actual words she used in Hebrew were *El Roi.* El Roi means the God that never sleeps, He sees, He is aware, He is the great, Omnipresent God.

Did you know that about God? Did you know he is the El Roi and that He is aware of what you are feeling and what you are going through? Hagar said, "Have I not, even here in the wilderness, remained alive after seeing Him (who has understanding and compassion)?" That truth is true for us. Lovers of God, we have to get past knowing the text of the Bible and knowing the truth of the letters and seek out the mysteries of God. What does that mean? It means that we don't just know all the accounts of the Bible. We aren't just full of head knowledge. It means that we are learning the character of God in relation to us. We can know in our soul how He responds to contrite and repentant hearts and refuses to deny them (Psalm 34:18). We can learn how He responds to hearts that are lost and broken and in the wilderness who thinks that if God really saw them would they even live? Would He be compassionate, or would He despise them as wrong and ugly? Would God *really* look on them with understanding and care? We can deeply know, not only in an intellectual way, but an experiential way, that He hears, He sees, and knows, and He still loves and still has an eventual good for us!

The wilderness parts of our journey can bring out fear in us. We don't have a lot of direction when our course sets out in a place that is so rough, wild, and with no signs that anyone else made it out alive or even went through this way. As much as we

{ HE IS LOOKING FOR YOU.
HE IS CARING FOR YOU
AND COMING AFTER YOU! }

don't like the discomfort of being in a foreign place without a lot of control, God is ever present and you can find Him in the wilderness. I was going to say if you're looking you'll see Him, but you know what? It isn't like that, is it? *He is looking for you.* He is caring for you and coming after you! He found not just Hagar, but others too! Moses found a burning bush when he went through the wilderness to Siani. Israel journeyed through the wilderness for 40 years. They weren't allowed to go to the Promised Land until their sin was dealt with; but they didn't get swallowed up by their enemies out there either! They were cared for. There was a cloud by day, a fire by night, and manna every day of that extended stay. The younger generation had a faith that was built in the steadfast care of God. They knew that He was going to give them the Promised Land. Jesus retreated into the wilderness to pray often, but it was during His 40 day fast in the wilderness that He overcame temptation and was released to begin His ministry into the Earth. There's purpose in the wilderness seasons and it won't last forever. Lysa Terkeurst explains the wilderness this way, "We have to walk through His process to get to God's fulfilled promise...it's the exact preparation you need."

This was true for Hagar too. In Genesis 21, again, Hagar found displeasure in Sara's sight. Hagar was laughing and Sara felt like it was mocking and disrespectful. Ironic too, that Sara laughed when she first heard the promise that she would carry a child in her old age. Isn't it so much easier to see others' shortcomings than our own? This laughter, whether it was mocking or not, is what sent Hagar and with her son, Ishmael, out into the wilderness again with just limited provision and no direction.

When the water in the skin was gone, she put the child under one of the bushes. Then she went and sat down opposite him a good way off, about the distance of a bowshot, for she said, "Let me not look on the death of the child." And as she sat opposite him, she lifted up her voice and wept. And God heard the voice of the boy, and the angel of God called to Hagar from heaven and said to her, "What troubles you, Hagar? Fear not, for God has heard the voice of the boy where he is. Up! Lift up the

boy, and hold him fast with your hand, for I will make him into a great nation." Then God opened her eyes, and she saw a well of water. And she went and filled the skin with water and gave the boy a drink. And God was with the boy, and he grew up. He lived in the wilderness and became an expert with the bow.
(Genesis 21:15-20)

The previous wilderness experience was the exact preparation that Hagar needed for this next season. We could say this time the situation looked even worse than the first! The first time, Hagar left on her own. This time she was told to leave and she couldn't come back. The first time, she was by a spring of water. This time she had no water and her son with her! But there is one crucial thing we need to see. This time, Hagar called out to the Lord! She might not have had eyes to realize the total promise, but she knew that God would hear her cry. He gave her a promise that He hears! That bit of information was all she needed. God answered her, He provided for her and the boy, and He told her that what she cares about most, her son, would become a great nation. *Hold your promise tight in your hand, Hagar! I've got this!! El Roi is aware and will help you in your time of need.*

{ GOD TAUGHT ME TO MEDITATE ON CERTAIN THINGS, THINGS THAT ARE WITHOUT A DOUBT, LIKE HIS CONSTANT CHARACTER AND THE GOODNESS AND MERCY THAT FOLLOWS. }

He will take your previous wilderness season and it will prepare you for when you find yourself in a different tight spot. When it's not just you this time, but others depending on you, the relational God will provide for you and those relationships you care so much about...He will give you water to give them too! Water, so that they may live, so that they may grow in the wilderness and become an expert in those tough conditions! Hagar's revelation from her previous season was the exact thing that Ishmael needed too, but would have never known how to retrieve it himself.

I've found myself walking through a spiritual situation similar to Hagar. I have been in the wilderness before and I've encountered God again and again as the God who hears, sees, and knows. In that place of uncertainty with the things around me, God taught me to meditate on *certain* things, things that are without a doubt, like His constant character and the goodness and mercy that follows. So, though there are times where things feel tense and uncertain, I can lean into the certain things that I know. "He works all things for the good of those who love Him." (Romans 8:28) There is purpose even in tension. Oftentimes, it isn't even so much about what is happening right now, but about where you are going. *"God, what is it You are needing to grow in me and what is it I need from this to take with me?"*

There was a time when over and over, I was "raising a hallelujah in the presence of my enemies," and praising through the wilderness because I knew it didn't end there. Though that may be, it was still draining and challenging every bit of my faith. My faith in God was not wavering, but sometimes that "count it all as joy" is replaced by a cry like Hagar, *"I know You are there God and You hear, but please don't let me look on the death of my promises. Did I hear You wrong or misunderstand? It's not Your fault, God, I know that. But me? This could definitely be my fault."* When you're focused on a relationship with God even in the wilderness, you hear His words!

One week, I was having a dialogue with God that was filled with more questions than praise. He was so good to answer me through a unique situation that only He could provide. That weekend I was at *The Send* gathering in Camping World Stadium in Orlando, Florida. It was such an incredible gathering of almost 60,000 believers who came together to worship God in unity and answer the call of bringing the gospel into the world. In Florida, standing directly under the sun on the field, we were hot! My brother, Austin, and I went to get water in the field where everyone was worshipping since they were still working out the flow of letting people in and out of the stadium. The line was probably 500 or more people long; so we were stuck there for a while. The water cost five dollars each and they were only taking cash. I only had enough money to get water for me and Anthony, but I knew we needed it; so I got in the long line with my brother. When I got about three people from the front, someone that I didn't see handed me $80 and said, "Can you get sixteen waters?" I had his money already in my hand and so I thought, *"Of course, I will."* I was thinking he just wanted to skip the line for his group, but I couldn't exactly blame him since the line was so long. Austin said, "Who was that? What did he say?" I told Austin that he asked me to get sixteen waters.

When I got to the front I asked for eighteen waters. The water guy placed both hands on the counter and let out an irritated sigh. He then looked to the side and grabbed an empty case and threw it on the counter and started tossing all the water to me so quickly. I was so glad that I didn't get yelled at by him. I was desperately trying to follow his nonverbal directions and pathetically put the waters in the case all wrong! I kept thinking, *"This is going to be so heavy! And I'm doing it wrong!"* I was laying them down instead of up, and half way through I realized it was probably going to be impossible to fit the waters in the torn plastic bag of a case that probably tightly held 20-30 bottles standing up. Here I was laying eighteen icy, sweating waters down like a frantic woman that was still hoping to not get yelled at by the water guy!

My brother must have been reading my mind and said, "Hey, don't get that I'm going to help you." Austin held the water for me and I started to look for the mysterious guy who gave me the money. I didn't see him in the first place so I didn't know how to find him. Confused, I asked God, *"Where is this guy? I don't want to walk off with all of his water!"* Finally, I heard the same voice that gave me the money say, "No, that's for others! Can you just give them out to whoever needs them? There's a lot of people who need water!"

Over the next five minutes, so many thankful people saw us and freely received water that they didn't have to stand in line or even pay for. God spoke to me the next day in worship— *"That's how it is right now—you know how to get water and how to wait on water. You know where to get it and that it is important to do so. You may only have a little resource in your hands, just enough, but just like that anonymous person did, I will put resources in your hands. I know that you'll obediently purchase water, no questions asked, and it'll be for others. You don't have to worry about what you didn't have a chance to think of...how will you hold this...how will you do this...who is this even for...or why. I will have people like Austin help you carry the weight, help you pass it out."*

One of the guys who asked for water said, "Can I Cash-App you?" Of course, I told him no because I didn't buy it! There were so many who said, "thank you" and "I needed that and I wanted that so bad." It was only obedience. There is a humbleness that comes from knowing you just went and freely got the water. You didn't purchase it. It wasn't even your idea. No one owes you a thing. Freely you've been given, so freely you give.

When God released the revelation of that experience, I could not help but feel so known and so seen. He gave me a tailor-made, real-life situation to show me why so many hurting hearts had been around me and coming to me at the same time. He spoke freedom over the fear that I wasn't doing it right or that I would have to carry it alone. He showed me that it would be exactly what others need. God knows and sees and wants to illuminate parts of the wilderness for you, and it isn't just for you but for others too!

"Then God opened her eyes, and she saw a well of water.
And she went and filled the skin with water and gave the boy a drink."
(Genesis 21:19)

HE SEES YOU

God wants to stay so current in relationship with you that you are talking to Him about whatever is going on and He is the One doing the eye-opening! He wants you to know He is in the wilderness with you and won't leave you or forsake you; so go ahead and raise a hallelujah! He will provide the water and revelation you need to get through.

When you feel cast out and with no place to go, call on the Name of the Lord, for He is mighty to save. When you find that you're in a wilderness, instead of crying and hiding, call out to God and remember the promises He has spoken over you. Train your heart to know that God is relational to you! He is close to you and He hears.

A SEEKING PRAYER
Father, today if we are in a wilderness we remind ourselves of how You've already revealed yourself to us. We remind ourselves how we've seen You before in the places of our uncertainty and how mighty it was when You showed up! How we cried out that we are known and seen by You. We know you, Lord, and we know Your ways towards us. You're a loving provider and we trust that You will highlight to us the exact tools we need to make it out of this experience. We know that we can call on You and You'll answer and You'll tell us great and marvelous things. We love You and we trust You! Thank you for not leaving us on our own to figure it all out. You lovingly guide us and we look to You!

A SOAKING SONG
Raise a Hallelujah by Bethel Music / Goodness of God by Bethel Music

CHAPTER TEN

REST

*"Six days work shall be done, but on the seventh day you shall have a
Sabbath of solemn rest, holy to the Lord. Whoever does any work on it
shall be put to death. You shall kindle no fire in all your dwelling
places on the Sabbath day."*
(Exodus 35:2-3)

With a tear-stained face, I listened to my friend speak what God had been saying
to her over the last week, "You are a warrior...God gave you the heart of a warrior, but even warriors need rest." Good friends are the ones who know what
it is like to stand firm, when all that's left to do is to stand, and to pray and to
contend but will still point you to rest. Even better are the ones who will reach out to
you later in the week and remind you that even warriors need rest. A word that God
gave to her and one she felt compelled to share with another warring heart.

Rest...to relax...to cease movement...to recover strength.

Even the strong, even the ones who go to
the well, who go to their Source need the habit of
rest; not just even them, especially them. In this
place of feeling so much, God began speaking to me
on what it means to be at rest. As someone who has
been dubbed "Miss Busy" ever since she was a pre-

> EVEN THE STRONG, EVEN THE
> ONES WHO GO TO THE WELL,
> WHO GO TO THEIR SOURCE
> NEED THE HABIT OF REST.

schooler and has continued in that manner well into motherhood, I find myself saying,
*"But HOW? I have the workload of Martha but the heart of Mary. I desire Your friendship God,
I desire to gaze at You, to recline, to be in a rested position, but aren't You the One who is bringing
all of this to me? The people, the hurts, the responsibilities, this beautiful life that You have
entrusted to me? Rest? But how?"*

I find myself between the tension of these two things, but in the tension *is
the growth*. Pay attention to the tension because it is a sign that there is something to
see and understand at a different level than you have previously discovered. God is not
put off by our questions. No, in fact, I know He is laughing. Laughing at me. Laughing like we laugh when we see our busy little preschoolers lamenting over all their
tasks! An old Yiddish proverb says, "Man plans and God laughs." No, He isn't making
fun of us or thinking our cares are not important. He isn't cruel. He is for us. We can

go back to His character, His Name, and have full assurance that all of His actions to-wards us are of love.

It is so important for us to look at what God says as freedom statements and not as restrictions. God laughs at us, playfully, as we are His very busy and very stressed out little children. He laughs at your enemies because though they try, they can not break you. He laughs at the hardest of obstacles because He knows in it you grow more assured in His faithfulness and more relentless in heart. Might He be softly and kindly laughing because He knows you need rest? Oh, what a bit of rest will do for you. Rest, my friend, isn't a restriction but is for your good.

> PAY ATTENTION TO THE TENSION BECAUSE IT IS A SIGN THAT THERE IS SOMETHING TO SEE AND UNDERSTAND AT A DIFFERENT LEVEL THAN YOU HAVE PREVIOUSLY DISCOVERED.

Often, I've had a toddler in my lap and have been combing their hair with my hands, while they are crying over frustrations, or their toys not working out, or an argument with their brother and I tell them, "Relax, babe, you're tired. This isn't truly this bad, and you're feeling this way because you need rest." Sometimes that toddler will feel so seen and melt into my embrace. Other times, that toddler will be so persistently trying to get out of my lap to grumpily and exhaustedly stand their ground. It's a funny sight when you, as their parent, know they need to rest, but they are determined to dig their heels in. Silas, as a one-year-old, would crash like a giant with a toy in hand, cheek pressed hard against the floor, booty high up in the air. I would laugh that he finally gave it up and wonder how that position and the cold tile floor could be more comfortable than just letting me hold him.

Rest is not for the weak, but for the warrior, child of God. You are not being benched, you are being made strong. You are recovering strength. On this challeng-ing week, I found myself in Exodus where Moses tells us that on our Sabbath, our rest is holy to the Lord. It is our sacred time and our gift for Him. God has been teach-ing me the spiritual truth that you can just never ever outgive the good Giver. What we actually intend to give God is His gift to us. Rest, that holy trusting, that command that was so serious, that you would be put to death if you didn't abide by it. Literally, because of the law, but also, truly, what happens, if you run, run, run, and work, work, work, 6 days turns into 7, but it doesn't stop there and it goes, goes, goes without rest? Friend, you would die. You would burn out. You would not be able to go on.

This command is not a restriction, but it is a freedom statement that says, *"I see you, you're doing good baby, you're trying so hard, and you know what? I'm so proud of you, but you need to rest now. It will actually come easier to you when you're rested. You'll think and see more clearly too."* Recover by sincerely shelving everything that is important to you on this day of hustle, or this day of urgency, and give that day and time to the Lord. You can trust that He cares for you. Do you see that? He cares for you so you don't have to. *For you,* as in "care that is given to you like a gift." *For you,* as in "you don't have to because He is doing it on your behalf." (1 Peter 5:7)

God speaking to me on rest would have been enough; but God knows me and wanted to make it even more clear. He knows that I may need to put the work and the achieving down; but that I still might try to kindle that fire in my home. It's so precious to me that it was worded just like that when I needed to hear it. He could have said, "Don't leave your house, don't clean everything, or catch up on laundry," but He said, "Don't even kindle a fire in all your dwelling places." And that week, that's exactly where I was at "kindling fires..."

kindling my passion in devotion...
kindling prayers for my hurting friends...
kindling knowledge and words to help...

Kindling isn't bad; no it's very good and necessary. We should fan into flame; but kindling several fires that are dwindling is very draining! God loves us enough to remind us to rest and to recover strength. He is gentle enough with us that He doesn't want us to toil to ignite fire every day. Do you think it is your kindling that is going to manufacture a miracle? Is He capable without you? Might He just be the One who will keep your fire going and going so that you could kindle another day? Let God hold you! Rest. Do you hear laughing? Not mocking, not belittling, but the true laughter of the joyful Father! God doesn't leave you or forsake you, you're relationally close to the Good Father. Might His laughter, be your laughter? And His joy becomes your joy! Oh to know you have victory! Even when it doesn't look like it, we know, we know, we know because we know Who the battle belongs to!

Rest does not mean retreating. It isn't abandoning your post or going silent or saying that you can't go forward. David told his soul to encourage himself in the Lord when it looked like he lost everything and a good portion of his mighty men left his side. Like David, we can also go to the One who owns the battle and say, *"God I know You own this battle. I'll encourage myself (give myself courage) knowing that the battle is Yours! I'll stand when You say stand, I'll contend when You say contend, and I'll rest when You say rest. I'll rest so deeply that I won't even kindle a thing and be assured that this rest is Your gift to me."*

TREASURE OF A RHYTHM OF REST

Rest. Let that word sink deep into you, whether it is your Sabbath or your Monday grind. No matter where you find yourself today, God has rest for you in it. Sometimes we have to choose the position of rest. We have to purposefully choose to put rest in the rhythm of our week and that's worship. That's prioritizing the position of peace that God desires for you. When we plan for these restful days, or even daily moments of rest, it impacts everything for the better.

If you've been on difficult ground and feel like you have had to be a warrior these days, know that God put that determination in you! That's a gift to be able to see the present realities and have a conviction in your spirit that says, *"No. No this is not how the story ends for me.*" God might have given you a holy stubbornness, but when it comes to rest, you have to relent. That act of rest will increase your trust and help you recover the necessary strength to stand your ground.

A SEEKING PRAYER

God, today we give You ourselves in worship. We choose rest over kindling any good thing. You are the One thing, the only thing of Worth to us! Whatever is weighing us down and challenging us to dwell there in thoughts or actions or in prayers or in meditations, we turn all of that down to rest at Your feet and choose trust. All our kindling and You could do it in an instant! Oh, how You must laugh because we are innocent children and oh how it must delight You to see us try so hard. All of that can wait, we choose to rest with You today, we can kindle another day, and we know it's going to be the best day. You're such a good Father!

A SOAKING SONG

Defender by Rita Springer

CHAPTER ELEVEN

THE FIRE

"The fire on the altar must be kept burning; it must not go out. Every morning the priest is to add firewood and arrange the burnt offering on the fire and burn the fat of the fellowship offerings on it."
(Leviticus 6:12 ESV)

Oh, Leviticus. The book in the Old Testament that even the most diligent of Bible readers feel is such a struggle to get through. So many rules, so many consequences, so many descriptions and situations. The last time I read Leviticus, I remember asking God to show something that would grow me. Surely, this book must be important even for today when it holds so much of the law within it. Yes, we are living in the New Testament and we are under grace, but Jesus came to fulfill the law, not to do away with it. His sacrifice fulfilled our sin debt, but have you ever considered what carefulnesses the children of God had to exercise in order to be righteous and holy unto the Lord? Those living under the law had to endure a heavy load of physical and mental pressure.

I am not saying that today we should feel the same pressure of religious duty or works. Perhaps though, there is a weighty place in our hearts, a place with depth of feeling, careful intent, and holy affection, that should hold importance to

> THE LEGAL REQUIREMENTS OF BEING PURE AND HOLY WERE NOT LIFTED.

us so that we can draw more and more near. Jesus made the way—yes, He did completely. You can't earn it. His way is an open gate, a torn veil with access to holiness that says you *may* come. However, the legal requirements of being pure and holy were not lifted. It is for our safety that a holy God allows us to be forgiven of sins and cleansed, but just as we have to physically wash the world off of us each day, we also have to be renewed spiritually day by day. Sacrifice *each day*. It makes me think of King David, a man after God's own heart, who brought the ark of God back to Jersuelum and *every* six paces He made a sacrifice (2 Samuel 6:13), not because he had to, but because it mattered that much to him! God's love towards us is freely offered. Has the magnitude of it all affected you so much that you just can't get over it?

When reading in Leviticus about altars and types of offerings, I remember thinking, *"This must be important, because this is what the people offered to God. But more than that, there is something in this that God must desire."* I don't know about you but my heart says, *"God if You desire anything, I want to give it to You."* How great is that thought! The

God of all, the great and compassionate One, the Giver of good things, the One who walks with us through mess, through heartache, through all the things that come at us because of our fallen world, the one who sent His Son to bridge the gap, *that* God could desire something that I could give. Isn't that totally crazy? *Who am I, that You think of me?* "For I know the thoughts I think toward you, says the Lord, thoughts of peace and not of evil, to give you a future and a hope." (Jeremiah 29:11)

While I know we are not under the law of old, something in me said, *"Well if You liked it then, God, I want to know the way to Your heart and delight now."* Perhaps, there's a secret, hidden treasure in there. Maybe that's what Moses, a friend of God who talked with God face to face, meant when he said, "I pray you, if I have found favor in Your sight, let me know Your ways so that I may know You [becoming more deeply and intimately acquainted with You, recognizing and understanding Your ways more clearly] and that I may find grace and favor in Your sight." (Exodus 33:13) To know Him is to love Him and to desire to know Him all the more! Wisdom says, *"I long to have grace and favor in your sight because I know You'll pull me a little closer!"*

There are five types of offerings mentioned in Leviticus 6. One is the Grain Offering, which was to honor God and to say, *"Thank you for all that's mine, I know it's from You!"* Today, we do this too! We bring our tithes, first fruits, and offerings, on top of what we normally give, and our gifts to missions and causes that God lays on our hearts. This includes offerings of time and service unto the house of God and towards the body of Christ. We can relate to the grain offering because it is similar to gifts we still give!

> *"Glorify God with all your wealth, honoring him with your very best, with every increase that comes to you. Then every dimension of your life will overflow with blessings from an uncontainable source of inner joy!"*
> *(Proverbs 3:9-10 TPT)*

There was a Peace Offering, given in thanksgiving as a way to say, *"Thank you, God, thank you for fellowship with You, and for Your goodness towards me."* This peace offering reminds me of our times of worship. When we come together in the house of God and open our services with songs , they are testimony and expression of how good God is to us, and how much His relationship matters to us! Peace offerings take place not just at church, but also any time and place you turn on worship music or use the sound of your own voice to sing, or declare, or praise God and thank Him for His peace towards you!

> *"In God we have boasted all the day long,*
> *And we will praise and give thanks to Your name forever."*
> *(Psalm 44:8 AMP)*

Oh give thanks to the Lord; call upon his name;
make known his deeds among the peoples!
Sing to him, sing praises to him;
tell of all his wondrous works!
Glory in his holy name;
let the hearts of those who seek the Lord rejoice!
(Psalm 105:1-3 ESV)

The Sin Offering impressed me because it was for all uncleanness, even for unintentional sin and thoughtlessness. It demonstrated the seriousness of sin, and said, *"If there is any unclean way in me, restore me to You!"* This practice in today's culture seems to have lessened in significance. Yes, we might search our hearts at the end of the message on a Sunday morning, or perhaps before communion, but the Sin Offering reminds us that even unintentional sin needs our acknowledgement. Sometimes, when we stand in the, "I love God, I believe in God, I know the Word" camp, we lose sight of the fact that we still fall short daily. Our head knowledge tells us that we are sinners saved by grace. Could it be, in our hearts we aren't acknowledging that on our best days, "Our righteousness is like rubbish!" (Philippians 3:8-9) Or as Isaiah said, "We put on our prized robes of righteousness, but they are like filthy rags." (Isaiah 64:6)

Absolutely, we must move from thinking of ourselves as sinners to knowing we are sons and daughters. The heart of a son or daughter wants to make his or her dad so proud, so pleased. It's like, *"Hey dad, can I make You more proud? Hey, did You see how much more I can toss off that I don't need, because truly all that I desire is in You and to be in Your place of delight!"* This heart posture is not a place of duty; it is not trying to earn anything, but it's from a heart that longs to be *pure* of heart. It's knowing that the Father wants us to stop putting on old, tattered robes and instead *remain* in His robes of righteousness—remain because we are the righteousness of Christ, and we can abide there, not because of our works but because of His. (2 Corinthians 5:21) We do not have to work for this righteousness, but we do have to choose to walk in it.

You will again have compassion on us;
you will tread our sins underfoot and hurl
all our iniquities into the depths of the sea.
(Micah 7:19 NIV)

The Guilt Offering was for sins against God and others—the ones we knew about and carried guilt and shame over. Thank goodness, that today we can bring our guilt before the Lord and He washes us clean! There is therefore now no condemnation for those who are in Christ Jesus. (Romans 8:1 ESV)

The offering that impressed me the most was the Burnt Offering, an offering that could be given at any time. It's sole purpose was for reconciling the relationship of God and man. It was for renewal. It was so special that the law required that the fire never go out; it was to burn continuously! It wouldn't even go out on the Sabbath because they would kindle extra on the sixth day to ensure it stayed burning. So much so that it is echoed in verse 13. This offering seemed to say,

> *"God, I want You.*
> *This offering is additional.*
> *This offering is voluntary.*
> *This offering is for renewal."*

It is to say, *"God, I already thanked you for who You are to me, for Your goodness, for Your blessings. God, I already drew the line that if there is any sin in me, I want it out. The sin I did know about, I placed on the altar already, but this is the one I want to keep burning and to never go out. Renew me, God. I return. I desire Your relationship most. My relational position to You is so very important to me, God, see my offering, on fire coming up to You. Let it please You. God, let it be such a sweet aroma up to You that You send Your fire down consuming my offering. I want You, God, and I know You want me too."*

"Every morning the priest is to add firewood and arrange the burnt offering on the fire and burn the fat of the fellowship offerings on it." (Leviticus 6:12) I got stuck on that word, *"fat."* Why is that important? Hebrews 12:1 dropped into my heart, "Let us strip off every weight that slows us down, especially the sin that so easily trips us up." The sin and the weight. We could reason that every sin is weight that holds us down as we run this race, but is every weight a sin? And what is weight if it is not fat? The fat goes on the altar too. I read this during our church's corporate fast and I felt it fully, stomach growls and all. I was in the process of denying my flesh from fat and some tasty things that in excess could weigh me down because of the pursuit of growing closer to God. This laying down of fat, or fasting, is not out of duty, but for a closer relationship with God.

Fasting, like other offerings, moves God's heart. God is not a man who should change. If He delighted in something in the Old Testament, then He does so now as well. If Jesus said, "When you give, when you pray, and when you fast..." and gave specific instructions on each in Matthew 6, then he must have expected us to pursue giving, praying, and fasting. Sometimes, it is necessary for us to put other types of fat on the altar too. Things that are just weight and slow us down as we pursue the One who is worth it all. The fat can take form in many ways, not just food. One time it was what I was watching on TV; a show with too much of a time commitment that was not glorifying God. It was fun and would suck me in, but it was making me slow—it was just fat. Another time, it was the number of conversations I was engaged in throughout the day that slowed me down from focusing my attention to where it was needed. There was so much noise in my ears and too much heaviness in my mind that I needed to change my availability from being available to all, to being only available to who God led me to for a season.

LOVE OFFERINGS

What slows you down in your relationship with God? Is it too much noise or busyness, too much entertainment or keeping up with every single thing going on in the

> THERE IS A CLARITY OF MIND AND HEART THAT COMES FROM LETTING GO OF WHAT YOU DIDN'T NEED IN THE FIRST PLACE.

world? It might seem difficult to cut fat and put it on the altar of our heart as an offering to God, but it gets easier and more liberating every time. When you experience the freedom of letting things go that are unhealthy for you spiritually, it feels amazing! There is a clarity of mind and heart that comes from letting go of what you didn't need in the first place. Lightening your load of excess will make you want to go on a hunt for sin and fat in your house! "Throwing things out" can be delightful when you gain the perspective of the greater peace and clarity that will come as a result. You might also be thinking, *"What if you throw out some things or offer up some stuff that God wasn't even going to require?"* Well, that just makes me think of another offering mentioned in the Old Testament—the Free Will Offering. This offering was voluntary and extra worship. God will receive that too! You can never give God too much. Keep tending the fire and don't let it ever go out!

What is so spiritually heavy that you're not able to focus on your pursuit of being relationally in tune with your Father? Quiet your heart and ask the reflective question, *"What do I not need?"* Ask God, *"Is there something in me that is making me a spiritually fat Christian?"* Timothy reminds us to be, "ready for every good work." Let us put it all on the altar of our hearts—thanksgiving, repentance, sin, and even the fat.

A SEEKING PRAYER
Oh God, could I offer You more? Is that possible? If it is, I want to offer You ALL. God, You alone are worthy of giving everything. I give You every hope, every thank you, every sin that is so undesirable when held before Your Holiness. Today, I give You even the things that are making me spiritually fat, spiritually slow to act, spiritually distracted from Your Voice. When I give You all, You never leave me empty handed; You give me ALL I could ever want when You give me You! Oh God, You are so worth it. Let the altar of my heart burn continuously. Let my fire never go out.

A SOAKING SONG
House of Prayer by Eddie James

CHAPTER TWELVE

I LOVE YOU TOO

My youngest child, Ruby, is a bossy little girl. This most likely stems from being the youngest and only girl with two older brothers. It is awfully funny when someone who is so little thinks they have something to prove or something to speak up about...*all the time.* Ruby, the gem of the family, likes to do things all by herself. Since things can be a little touch and go if they are not to her very own liking, we tend to let her. For a little person, she is very capable! Oftentimes, her achievements lead her to feeling very accomplished and she will snuggle up and say, "I love you," completely content with her job well done. When she was three years old, she had the funniest habit of telling me, "Hey mom, I love you," all day long. Sometimes, it seemed as if she was just calling out to find out where I was, so she filled the silence with, "Hey, I love you!" If I responded with, "I love you," then she would echo again, "I love you!" If I replied again with, "I love YOU," her voice would get a little edgy as she said, "IIIIIIIIII love YOU," then she would wait.

It took us a little while, but we eventually realized that she was waiting for us to reply with, "I love you TOO!" This little bossy-pants actually had a point. The proper response when someone tells you that they love you is to reply, "I love you too." It acknowledges that the other person loves us too, and not just that, but that they loved us first. Or at least, they said it first!

One evening, I was talking to God and telling Him that I love Him and the Holy Spirit pricked my heart and said, *"No, no, Brooke...you love Him TOO."* And in that moment, I was filled with overwhelming love because that's right, *"I love Him too!!"* God is love (1 John 4) and He first loved. (1 John 4:19) He is constantly loving and showing his love to me in overwhelming ways allllllll throughout my day—alllll throughout my every single day. *"But God demonstrates his own love for us in this: While we were still sinners, Christ died for us."* (Romans 5:8) When we didn't even know Him, He gave His son. God made a way for us! When I was far off and didn't even know His voice, He still would show love and care to me. One of our loving God's characteristics is that He is omnibenevolent. This means that He is perfectly good. God is full of unlimited goodness all the time and in all the ways. He is the ultimate good and apart from him nothing could be considered good!

Exodus 34 reminds us that He is abounding in goodness! When we begin to realize that we are in the hands of a loving God, that our cry of "I love you" is in response to all of the goodness He shows us—not just when we draw close to Him, but all along—it's kind of overwhelming in the best way. You begin to realize that not only was He good in this circumstance, but also this one, and that one too. It begins to lead you down a list of provisions, kindnesses, and mercies shown again and again! Knowing that you are so loved by such a good God begins to produce a thankfulness in your heart that says, *"I love You too! It was You all along. You've always been with me!"* Psalm 23:6 says, "Surely goodness and mercy shall follow me all the days of my life; and I will dwell in the house of the Lord forever." As His children, we are loved and surrounded by both His goodness and His mercy!

> KNOWING THAT YOU ARE SO LOVED BY SUCH A GOOD GOD BEGINS TO PRODUCE A THANKFULNESS IN YOUR HEART THAT SAYS, "I LOVE YOU TOO! IT WAS YOU ALL ALONG, YOU'VE ALWAYS BEEN WITH ME!"

I can't ignore the fact that we face some situations that are very hard to see any possible good. I get that; I see you. Sometimes, in our fallen and dark world, yes, we walk through situations that seemingly have no possible markings of good to be seen. Where was the good God then? My friend, I see you!

Do you understand what I'm saying?

I see *you* and I hear *you*
because *you* have survived!
You are a survivor!

Whatever surrounded you did not get the final word because it was surrounded by God. God takes the victim and makes them the victor. No matter what pages are in the book of your past, the ones that you would like to rip out or burn— your story has not ended! Those pages are not the last word. You may feel like you are still standing on the battlefield and you have done all you can do. Just stand. Ephesians 6:13 says that when you have done everything, stand. Stand on your faith and know that there is so much more good to be had and so much more to be written! "I remain confident of this: I will see the goodness of the LORD in the land of the living." (Psalm 27:13)

"Have you considered my servant Job?" Have you heard the story of Job who was a righteous man who lost everything? There is a whole book in the Bible about Job and his life, one that we can learn a lot from. Job was blameless, honest, and turned away from sin. (Job 1:7) He was a wealthy good man who loved God. He had great kids who got along so much that they were friends who got together. He even prayed for his kids, "as this was his regular custom." God delighted in Job and He loved him. The accuser challenged God that Job only was this way because God had put a hedge of protection and blessing surrounding him. God allowed Job to be tested with the limitation that he couldn't be killed, only tested.

The Spark Notes version tells that on the next day: Job lost his oxen, donkeys, camels, and servants to an attack. His sheep and more servants died because of fire on the same day, and while he was processing these losses; another person came to tell him all his sons and daughters died from what sounded like a tornado destroying the house they were in. At this, Job got up and tore his robe and shaved his head. Then he fell to the ground in worship and said, "Naked I came from my mother's womb, and naked I will depart. The Lord gave and the Lord has taken away; may the name of the Lord be praised." In all this, Job did not sin by charging God with wrongdoing. (Job 1:20-22)

So Job lost all He had in a day. Like everything. And He still found it in him to praise God. The dialogue between God and Satan continued and God said, "Did you see Job and how he still holds fast?" And the accuser replied, "Well, that's because you didn't let me touch his body." So God said, "Fine go ahead but you cannot kill him." (Paraphrase Mine) Job was tormented with sores, peeling skin, worms, scabs, unending pain, and fever. Job's wife told him that he should curse God and just die, but the Bible tells us that in all this, Job still did not sin.

Throughout the whole book, we find Job enduring every type of hardship one could go through. He lost everything, everyone, and his body was hurting fiercely. You better believe, his mind and spirit were too. The next chapters outline how Job felt misery, bitterness, longing for death, hopelessness, lack of peace, no rest, terrifying visions, and shame. He had a broken fear of God because he didn't understand God anymore. Job's plans were completely broken. He had no dignity, and even his friends were telling him that he must have done something horribly wrong—that it must be all his fault. Eliphaz, Bildad, and Zophar, Job's closest friends, all take turns telling him what they think; why this must have happened. They all accuse him of sinning and that he has been cursed. A lot of chatter. If your friends are telling you their opinions on some deep things you are walking through, but they haven't talked to God to find out what He says about it all, then all that chatter is just noise.

Job speaks up and talks about how awful he feels. Rightfully so. And how disillusioned he is about God's ways. There is one person who hasn't spoken yet, Elihu.

"Now Elihu had waited to speak to Job because the others were years older than he. And when Elihu saw that there was no answer in the mouths of these three men, he burned with anger."
(Job 32:4-5)

Elihu speaks up in the next few chapters not agreeing with the others' view that before Job began suffering he had sinned. Elihu had a burning fire in him that made him stand up and despite his young age, say, *"Since you began suffering, you have sinned."* The other friends were telling Job that it must have been that you aren't as good as you say, there must be something in secret; but Elihu says, "NO, NO maybe you were fine then, but YOU CAN NOT question my God like that, your thoughts are leading you down a sinful way *now*." Our imagination is very serious to God. If you are imagining that you have no hope, no help, that is offensive to the God of everlasting love. Elihu tells Job, "It's not something you previously did, but it's what you are saying and thinking *right now* that is a problem." Elihu is controversial and some say that it is his immaturity that causes him to speak out of turn and to go off at the mouth. While I agree that Elihu's youth might have impacted his delivery and might not have been an accurate discernment of Job's heart, Elihu's words provide an important heart check for anyone who has been through suffering and is doubting the goodness of God or His love towards them. Elihu reminds that God does speak through pain. (Job 32-33) He says that Job has accused God of not giving him a fair trial and that God is a God of justice. He questions these older men and asks Job if he really thinks there is no point to try and please God? (Job 34:9 MSG) He reminds them that God is aware of everything and nothing could be hidden from Him. Elihu argues that God will hold the wicked accountable. More than that, Elihu speaks of how God is worthy of our righteous living and we can not criticize Him but we should revere Him.

What I love about Elihu, is that he is YOUNG and burning with fire for God. He can't sit back and let those older than him, or maybe even those more righteous than him, accuse God of not being faithful and just. Maybe he needs to fine tune his delivery and maybe as a passionate and burning one, I can relate to that. I have found that I might have the right words or perspective but delivery is key. Not everything spouted off in a righteous anger lands well. Proverbs 12:18 says, "The words of the reckless pierce like swords, but the tongue of the wise brings healing." (NIV) When dealing with people going through the hardest of seasons and who are as fragile as Job, we can not afford to have reckless words. Even truth that is delivered recklessly will be like a sword that is thrust forward, hitting the very person that needs the ministry of words that are healing.

After Elihu speaks, and boy does he speak for 6 chapters, NO ONE else says a word, not Eliphaz, Bildad, Zophar, or Job. The next one to speak is God, Himself! Out of a whirlwind the Lord answers Job and tells him of His mighty works and care for creation and that He has not forgotten him. He tells Job that his three friends missed it and that Job should actually pray for them. He does not address Elihu but there is something about when you begin to talk about God rightly and you proclaim His goodness, He draws near! God restored Job double of every single thing He lost. Not just restored to give again, not just double, but the quality of what He had was greater. The revelation of God changed everything for Job. His first set of children were known for their fun and their partying and perhaps why Job was always making sacrifices on their behalf to make sure they were in good standing with God. The second set of children had names that spoke of their great character and the status of his beautiful daughters were equal to that of their brothers. Daughters receiving equal inheritance was a tremendous honor that was not common in that time period and displays the greatness of the restoration! God gave Job a long life, honor, and fruitfulness!

Some people look at Job's story and have trouble with it because they can't reason why God would let a good person suffer. Isn't that a question we hear a lot? If

God is so good, then why do bad things happen to good people? God is not subject to our reasoning. "For my thoughts are not your thoughts, neither are your ways my ways, declares the Lord. For as the heavens are higher than the earth, so are my ways higher than your ways and my thoughts than your thoughts." (Isaiah 55:8-9)

RELY ON WHAT YOU KNOW

God was not playing games with Job; God loved Job fiercely and was proud of Job and the way he was living. Sometimes when we find ourselves where nothing seems certain and no one can really speak words of healing to us, we have to rely not on what we feel but what we know. We can know that there is no amount of pain that is too great for God to heal. We can know that God loves us. God cares for us. God will outdo Himself making things go well for you! (Deuteronomy 30:9) Suffering can refine us when we turn to God and lean into the word that He has for us! We can trust Him, He will never leave us or forsake us. (Hebrews 13:5b) Suffering can produce holiness when we find ourselves with God when all other things fall away. God is good and loving and He will use all the things in your life to bring glory. Glory, beauty, testimony! Double for the trouble!

> { WE HAVE TO RELY NOT ON WHAT WE FEEL BUT ON WHAT WE KNOW. }

"Instead of your shame there shall be a double portion;
instead of dishonor they shall rejoice in their lot;
therefore in their land they shall possess a double portion;
they shall have everlasting joy."
(Isaiah 61:7)

A SEEKING PRAYER
Let this be the cry of our hearts, not simply I love You, but I love You too! I acknowledge You in all the loving ways You come to me. Even in hard times, I know You are with me. You are good to me. In all the ways, You say it often. Again, and again, I hear You say to me, "I love you, you are Mine, you are my child." I can know that You didn't cause my suffering, but Your Hand was preserving me. My story did not end there. My story does not end in this fallen world because You even say You are preparing a place for me! You are a good, good Father who is constantly saying to me, "I love you, I always have, and it's with an everlasting love." I will see goodness and mercy, they will follow me all the days of my life, because You are with me.

A SOAKING SONG
Always Good- Hannah McClure

CHAPTER THIRTEEN
BREATH IN MY LUNGS

I don't think there is anything that we want to get more right than taking care of our children. That desire is in us because it is a reflection of our own good Father. We, however, are very familiar with our own human limitations knowing that it's just impossible to do it right, all the time, on our own. This is something that I found out to be true from the very beginning with my first baby, Silas. At the end of the first trimester of my pregnancy, I started bleeding heavily. Blood is never something you want to see with pregnancy and there was so much blood that we went straight to the emergency room. I remember praying the whole way there, but also being so scared to breathe. I felt like I was willing my body to keep whatever blood it needed inside and begged God, *"Please no."*

When we arrived, they did an ultrasound and we saw the little bean-like baby in my uterus moving about and the doctor came and told me these miracle words, "Your cervix is closed." I could barely believe it because I saw so much blood. It is hard to argue with what we saw and I kept asking if he was sure everything was okay. The ER doctor explained to me that there was a strong heartbeat and that my cervix was closed. He said my body had threatened to abort the fetus, but that whatever was causing the bleeding had stopped. He then put me on bedrest until I could see my doctor. His words that *my body* had threatened abortion caused me to feel so betrayed by my body.

When I saw my regular doctor, he was kind, but didn't really have answers. He just said that sometimes these things happen and it could've been a number of reasons. It didn't exactly fill my heart with peace, but I think this situation awakened me to the fact that this whole miracle of a baby was in God's hands, not mine at all. I was only twenty-three years old, and honestly a little terrified after that experience, so much so that I had a bit of trouble connecting to Silas when he was still in my womb. I remember I would pray for him, especially while driving to my job at the Nature's Market, but talking to him was not something I would do. I was too scared. What if something like that night at the emergency room happened again?

When my due date came, I was so excited. I did not think I would go past it because after all it's a due date! I must have known because on my due date they actually sent me to the hospital to prepare for induction. Again, my body was showing signs of letting me down. I had preeclampsia. I was so naive. I didn't really think that I needed to be concerned because it was my due date after all. Babies that make it to their due date are healthy and are on time so this made sense. We went home and got our things and couldn't believe that this was the day we were going to become parents! Naturally, we decided we needed to swing by Chick-fil-A for breakfast and then headed to the hospital. I didn't realize that preeclampsia was a thing that needed to be addressed in my body and that it was affecting baby Silas. The next day, a distressed Silas Gage was born via c-section. I heard him cry out once he was born and my heart crumbled in gratitude. That cry, that voice was uniquely *my* son's.

It was the only bit of Silas that I would connect to that day because before they could place him in my arms, I heard lots of talking back and forth saying, "The baby isn't breathing well," and "Dad, do you want to stay with the baby?" I was fading and telling Anthony, "Go, go with him. Don't leave him!" I would not get to see the baby that I gave birth to that day. I woke up the next morning feeling empty. I didn't feel my baby in me anymore and I had no idea where he was. Anthony assured me that Silas was okay and just needed a little extra help breathing and he was in the NICU. He told me that once I was okay, we could go see him. Anthony assured me that it would be okay, Silas was so beautiful, and our parents had made it to Florida.

I felt so confused because the NICU was for babies who were born early or were there because there were problems in pregnancy—not babies born on or after their due date. I had never even thought for a minute that Silas would go there, and again, I felt like my body, now full of pain, physically and emotionally, had failed me.

For the next six days, Silas remained in the NICU for a tear in his lungs. It was really tough because these weren't the experiences I had prepared for. No one told me to expect that the first time seeing my baby might be a blurry picture on a phone. I didn't know I would be told by a nurse to not touch him and only when permitted to may I touch his tiny foot. There wasn't a baby placed on my chest to learn how to feed, and I wasn't prepared for learning how to produce milk on a pump. This was all wrong, but at the same time I knew that Silas was in God's hands, and that I could trust that. I could trust Him.

Every day they were telling us that if the tear didn't repair, Silas would have to have surgery. Every day at 6 a.m. they would do an x-ray and Anthony and I, on a completely different floor of the hospital, would hold hands and pray that God would heal Silas' lungs. We would dedicate Silas back to God and ask Him to take care of our baby. On the sixth day, the hole vanished and on the seventh day we got to take our baby home! Another miracle concerning Silas written in my heart!

The day after Silas turned three, his baby brother, Ezra Arrow, was born via VBAC. God looked kindly on the girl who thought her body failed her and showed her that He cared about that too. When the boys went to their well checkup two months later, I mentioned to their doctor that I wanted to show her a video of how Silas sounded when he slept each night to see if it was normal. She said it was not, and from there we saw an ENT who sent us to do a sleep study. The ENT called us back the next day and asked if we could do surgery two days later. They told us that his sleep study showed that Silas stopped breathing more than 63 times during the six-hour study. I could barely believe it. I was just adjusting to having a brand new baby, and now my three-year-old needed immediate surgery for not breathing! I was barely getting over being scared about parenting Silas and was already transferring those fears to knowing what the new baby needed. Again, it was not in my hands, but in God's. And again, God was faithful.

He spoke comfort to my heart when I was afraid and freaking out that Silas had not been breathing well. The Holy Spirit reminded me that yes, when Silas' breath caught 63 times in that study, and also every other time that he wasn't breathing, that it was God who had started his breath again. Each and every time, God breathed into Silas. He did it, without fail, before I even knew there was a problem. I could trust Him.

Everything with Silas and his breathing remained fine for a long time after that. You can imagine my surprise two years later, during the middle of the tough year that was 2016, when Silas began to wake us up with asthmatic attacks. The sound of Silas sucking in air and choking and not being able to catch his breath isn't one that I'll ever forget. It began one night, and just continued. When he would wake in the morning, Silas was in a daze and was pretty non-responsive. Even though he was five, Silas would fall asleep exhausted when we were driving and the vein in his neck would bulge, his breathing would stutter, and he would gasp for air.

In the middle of everything else we were facing, Silas' breathing was a problem again. My spirit was crushed and *my breath* felt caught in my throat. Again, we began doctor appointments and sleep studies. It was clear that there was a problem and worse than before, so much so, that his body wasn't fully getting oxygenated. The doctor said things like, "This time he didn't breathe more than 80 times and the apnea is more severe than last time." He told us that Silas needs a CPAP for 8 weeks so that we can be confident that he will wake up from anesthesia. *The doctor thought it was too risky to do the surgery then because he wasn't sure that Silas would wake up.* I was devastated that we were facing this again, but now in a tough year without my friends and not just with a baby brother, but now with a baby sister, Ruby Autumn, too.

If you've ever been standing back on the battlefield of something that you thought was already over and won, you know, how defeated I felt. It made me think of the children of God who survived Egypt, that God brought the victory and made it through the wilderness. Then when they were about to inherit the land that is theirs, they were told they would have to drive out other foes first. What? I thought we were at the end of our troubles; but here we are again, another battlefield that seems awfully similar to the first.

Discouragement begins to creep in and doubt tries to cloud the fact that we have the victory of the past battle, and we will have the victory in the next because God is with us.

"The Lord is good,
A strength and stronghold in the day of trouble;
He knows [He recognizes, cares for, and understands fully]
those who take refuge and trust in Him."
(Nahum 1:7)

Just like in other times of darkness, the Holy Spirit gave us words to stand on during this time.

"I lie down and sleep; I wake again, because the LORD sustains me."
(Psalm 3:5)

"When you lie down, you will not be afraid; when you lie down,
your sleep will be sweet."
(Proverbs 3:24)

Precious words like these held us up during this time. We would speak these scriptures over Silas each night and we would trust that God was taking care of him. One day when I was having a particularly hard time with all that we were going through and anxiously waiting for the day of surgery, I heard singing coming from Silas' room. My five-year-old was sitting on his bed

{ "WHEN THE SON WAS LIFTED UP, HE PUT NEW BREATH INSIDE MY LUNGS." }

with his back to me and he was singing and playing. What stopped me was the words that he was singing. Silas was singing a Leeland song that goes, "When the Son was lifted up, He put new breath inside my lungs." Again and again, his nasally obstructed voice sang, "He put new breath inside my lungs!" I can't tell you how this made me stop and hear God speaking. I can't even begin to tell you how it made me feel to hear my little guy singing that over his body. I can't tell you how much I knew God was telling me that, *"He was the One who puts new breath inside Silas' lungs again and again and to not worry."* God speaks and He even speaks through children's praises!

"You have built a stronghold by the songs of babies.
Strength rises up with the chorus of singing children.
This kind of praise has the power to shut Satan's mouth.
Childlike worship will silence the madness of those who oppose you."
(Psalm 8:2 TPT)

If we are listening—oh how we will hear Him! I called Anthony crying and told him what Silas was singing and he told me he had just got in his car while praying for Silas and the Housefires song "Life Is A Gift" happened to be playing with the lyrics, "Every breath is a gift from You. We breathe in deep Your mercy!"

TREASURE OF HE GUARDS ALL THAT IS MINE

"LORD, you alone are my inheritance, my cup of blessing.
You guard all that is mine."
(Psalm 16:5 NLT)

God guards all that is mine. All that He has given to me. How freeing it is to know it's not up to my body! How wonderful to know it's not up to me. My good, good Father guards all that is Mine for me. Anxiety just melts when I consider that. Fear has to submit to a greater Fear of the Lord. For me, this verse just disarms every other idea that would try to exalt itself above the goodness and care of my Beloved. I want to speak this treasure over you today and for you to know, as I do, that the Lord guards all that is yours!

A SEEKING PRAYER
God thank you for speaking. Thank you for giving us words that we can cherish from the praises of children! God when we face battles that look similar to ones that we have faced before, let us remember that You delivered us last time! Won't you be faithful to do it again? Do it again, God! We know that You are for us! That everything that You have planned will be for our good. When we don't know what to do, our eyes are on You!

A SOAKING SONG
Son Was Lifted Up by Leeland / Life is A Gift by Housefires

THE KING IS HERE

May 2016 marked the start of the second breathing battle, with the surgery scheduled for October 7th. I was learning to trust God and submit anxiety to Him. Anxiety was yelling so many things at me. *"How long has this been going on? The time between each appointment is taking too long. They are telling you that Silas isn't breathing and making you wait days and days, just knowing that. Paperwork and process are keeping you from the needed CPAP machine. Every day that they are delaying is a day of uncertainty for you. How can you sleep knowing that he isn't breathing and the machine to help isn't here yet? You are no one's priority."* In this place, I was learning Psalm 94:19 (CEV). "And when I was burdened with worries, you comforted me and made me feel secure."

A couple of days before surgery, the first Category 5 hurricane in eleven years to threaten my town began to be all that anyone was talking about. Hurricane Matthew was moving towards a direct hit of our beachside town on the very same Friday that Silas' surgery was scheduled. We couldn't believe it. We felt defeated. The surgery that could only be scheduled once a month had to be rescheduled and moved from October to December. This meant two more months of waiting, praying, and sleeping with the CPAP machine every night. If this wasn't enough, the Weather Channel was strongly predicting Hurricane Matthew to directly hit the barrier island that we live on!

Matthew was also the first hurricane that we faced since moving to Florida. The Weather Channel described the image of the hurricane right off our coast as resembling a demonic skull inching closer to directly hitting Indian Harbour Beach where our home, church, and community are located. They kept talking about how crazy it was, but for me, it didn't feel crazy at all, but exactly what was happening. We evacuated to family in Tennessee and early on Friday morning when Matthew was expected to make landfall, we waited, we prayed, and watched the radar on the TV as Matthew, just off our coast unexpectedly and quickly dropped from a Category 5 to a 3. It was skirting up our harbour, never making land in our community. As the hurricane bumped closer and closer, it was like there was something preventing it from moving west and instead pulled it north. It changed paths before our eyes while we were praying and watching the radar.

"God stilled the storm, calmed the waves, and he hushed the
hurricane winds to only a whisper."
(Psalm 107:29 TPT)

"When I (God) said, 'This far you may come and no farther;
here is where your proud waves halt.'
(Job 38:11 NIV)

God was so good to us just like he had been in many other situations! God, my deliverer! Our home was spared. On the way home, we saw evidence of Matthew all around when we looked at the houses, fences, and trees. All of the fences surrounding our rental house fell, but our plastic kiddie pool that we forgot to bring in was still resting on our house! God spoke to our hearts encouragement about how His protection is like a blanket of protection. When we got back home we rejoiced; we began thanking God for every single thing in our house. We had thought we weathered the storm, but it wasn't even close to over. The very next evening, a very special person to us died suddenly.

The news that night left me utterly raw and broken before the Lord. Anthony and I quietly put the children to bed, not ready to tell them, not really believing it ourselves. I went into our guest room and closed the door and called my mom and dad and just cried to them. One of the hardest parts about living so far from family are times like these. We had just celebrated the victory of our home being sustained *hours ago.* We were still contending for Silas' healing, and this news crumbled us. We were not ready for this.

We were devastated and mourning the loss of someone whom we loved deeply. The kind of person who the Holy Spirit used to speak gently to me, the one who saw me and cared for me, and celebrated the words that God had given me. The kind of person that no matter what walls I had up, the very sound of their voice tore them down and ushered God's love in. She loved my kids as if they were her own and fulfilled a familial role when there was no one in close proximity who could do it to the degree that she could. That night, I was grappling with how she was gone, laying in bed crying silently on a night that I should have still been celebrating being home and looking forward to our Ruby turning one the next morning. Ruby still woke many times during the night for feeding and cuddles, but that night she slept through the entire night. It felt like angels must have been rocking her and God must have been holding me all through that night.

The next day, a close friend came and took the boys to play so I could grieve alone. I put the now one-year-old Ruby down for a nap and turned worship music on to drive out the depression filling my house. Kim Walker began to sing *The King Is Here.*

The King is here, the King is here
You're alive inside of me
The King is here, the King is here
Love will never ever leave

I began to hear it as if God, Himself, was singing it to me, *"Brooke, the King is Here, the King is Here!! You can worship, you can praise, you can rejoice, for the King is here! You're living to proclaim the King is here!"* I listened to that song on repeat for hours. My heart, raw and broken, before the Lord. If walking through night seasons has taught me anything it is that God *can*

> GOD CAN WORK WITH
> RAW AND OPEN HEARTS.

work with raw and open hearts. Those hearts are honest! Those hearts aren't afraid of drawing close to Abba and spilling it out. They fear Him, yes, but they can know their position of love with Him.

David said in Psalm 51, "The sacrifices of God are a broken spirit; a broken and contrite heart, O God, you will not despise." Jesus told his disciples, "But everyone my Father has given to me, they will come. And all who come to me, I will embrace and will never turn them away." (John 6:37) He will not turn you away in rejection! In this heavy and dark season, God spoke to me that, *"The King is here,"* and I knew if the King was here, I could endure this season or any season as long as I knew He was there.

EVEN IN THE NIGHT SEASON

"I will bless the LORD who guides me; even at night my heart instructs me."
(Psalm 16:7 NLT)

And He *was* there. God continued to meet me in my secret place, in the quiet times before Him. He met me in His Word. He met me in worship songs and in messages at church. He didn't just meet me, He guided me. He told me to slow down my pace and only do the necessary and stay close to Him because He was close to me. This

> THE DARKNESS REVEALED HOW
> BRIGHTLY HIS LIGHT SHINES AND
> HOW THE DARKENSS COULD NOT
> OVERTAKE ME WHEN I HID MYSELF
> IN HIM AND DREW COURAGE IN
> KNOWING, "THE KING IS HERE!"

season didn't stay dark forever, God broke through. Silas' second surgery eventually happened and it resolved his breathing issues—100%! God taught me so much in this night season that helped me hold strong to faith in future trials. The darkness revealed how brightly His light shines and how the darkness could not overtake the light! It could not overtake me when I hid myself in Him and drew courage in knowing, "The King is here!"

It doesn't matter how dark, messy, or long the season has been. The King is with you. He wants you to know that. Even if you feel like what you're going through is your fault, it doesn't matter. He has not left your side. Sure, there may be hardships to walk through because of consequences. Yes, there are times where it is not because of anything you did and it is just a hard season where you are learning and apprehending treasure that will never leave you because of the significance of this time and the magnitude of that trial. The King is here. Ask Him to reveal to you how near He is and the treasure of His Words. He will speak to you about where you are now and where you are going.

A SEEKING PRAYER

Jesus, I thank you that you are the friend that sticks closer than a brother and that you sent us the Holy Spirit as comforter! Oh, how I felt Your comfort in this season and how I pray that You breathe comfort into anyone who might be in a dark period! The darkness tried to put out the light but it could not extinguish it. King Jesus, You have overcome the world! Our good Father reigns and His eye is ever on us! He will protect us and He will sustain us. Remind us today that there is nowhere we can go that we will escape You! I say, "Surely the darkness will hide me and the light becomes night around me, even the darkness will not be dark to you; the night will shine like the day, for darkness is as light to you." (Psalm 139) God, if the person reading this finds themselves in a season like this today, light up the night, make the hidden treasures of this time shine bright in the dark!

A SOAKING SONG

The King is Here by Kim Walker-Smith

CHAPTER FIFTEEN

PUZZLE PIECES

My sister and her boys spent two weeks with us during the summer of 2020 so that we could quarantine together while the whole world was waiting for the Coronavirus to stop threatening life as normal. It was the perfect plan because her house was undergoing renovation and staying home together allowed lots of playtime for the cousins. When she was with us, we started working on bright 1,000 piece puzzles. Because of the virus and people staying home so much, puzzles were sold out everywhere, both in store and online, and that only added to the excitement of having a few of our own.

We found ourselves letting the kids play and watch movies, while we were enjoying our coffee and conversations and, of course, working swiftly and efficiently putting together our masterpiece puzzle. There was something that just felt so right about putting together 1,000 little pieces to make a complete and beautiful picture when everything else in the world seemed completely upside down. Fear has a way of making life feel like a million little pieces, ugly, out of order, upside down, and not making sense at all. Focusing on putting together these physical pieces felt like a protest against fear and a declaration that my home was a home of peace and order, no matter what chaos loomed around us.

The little cousins were contently doing whatever they wanted because we were distracted and pleased with our puzzle making. As long as everyone was happy, the mamas were happy too! My sister and I got a little bit obsessed and did several puzzles over the course of their stay; but the desire to acquire the best and brightest 1,000 piece challenges was still lingering after she left. Every few days over the next couple of weeks, I would check the store or the online marketplace and they were always sold out or didn't have ones I liked.

One day, I found the most perfect one that I had ever seen on our local online marketplace! It was an "I love Florida" puzzle, and if you know me you know I *love* Florida and this one had so many fun images and words related to all things Florida! And most importantly, it was one that was sold out! I was so excited and immediately knew that I needed it. I needed to start this puzzle, and binge work on it beginning to end, ignoring the state of the world, then all would be right, especially because this one was a Florida-themed one. I'll blame my displaced feelings on the effects of 2020! I contacted the puzzle man and to my dismay, his wife had already sold it. *Whommp Whommp.*

A few days after my precious Florida puzzle was taken (yes mine, I had already felt like it was mine), Anthony and I were celebrating our 11-year anniversary

WORDS ARE TREASURES | 79

on a little getaway. We decided to do some shopping at an outdoor mall and while we were walking by a toy store that had it's doors open, something caught my eye! I shouted and pointed because I saw the brightest 1,000 piece puzzles in the center display! I wanted several, but I knew Anthony might think that I was a little crazy (he had yet to join me in my obsession;) so I asked the clerk if they happened to have the "I love Florida" puzzle. He said, "We do....hmmm, no, not there, wait. We do have one, in the window display!" Ahhh! I was so excited and felt like I won the lottery. The very last one. The only one!

Anthony, of course, was happy for me, and also after 11 years of marriage was used to my ridiculous obsessions. He sometimes will ask me, "Is this like the essential oils, or the cloth diapers, or when we were vegan, or the books?" And I'll have to answer, "Yes," so that he can know how important these kinds of things are.

Our trip was wonderful and once we were home, I waited about three days before it was the perfect time to start working on the "I love Florida" puzzle. With intense social issues like injustices and riots pressing hard in our world, the virus climbing and everyone not sure what to do, and some other closer-to-home-things weighing heavily—the puzzle was the perfect two-day distraction. I would joke that this was the very best puzzle ever and that we would need to put it in our will to leave our great grandchildren so that they would know we lived and loved Florida and that we even put it together during the crazy year of 2020.

I worked throughout that day and the next. One of the kids would come and help with a section of the puzzle or hold up a piece and look at it and another one would talk about something they saw on it or a Florida memory that popped in their mind. Later, Anthony would sit down and work on a section that was too hard to resist. Finally, when it came to the last few pieces and the kids were in bed, we knew we were going to finish it!

We fit the last couple of pieces in place and like a cruel joke there was *one piece* missing in the middle. All that effort and time and a piece was missing out of the glorious puzzle! We looked all around the room we were in and around the other rooms but it was no use. Anthony said that we could still put the puzzle in our will and just write a note to why there was a missing piece. I had to tell him, "No, that was unacceptable and I will pray about it and I think God will help me find it." I really, was fairly sure, not certain, that I didn't throw it away by mistake. How do you like that assurance?

My faith was waning a little bit because, well, I could have easily thrown it away. I'm often distracted and it was just a silly puzzle. Earlier in the year, I had lost one of my favorite earrings and I thought for sure that I would find the missing one, but I didn't. What if it turned out just like that? It was my fault for being silly and so involved about something trivial when so much was going on that actually mattered. Still, we prayed and asked God to help me find it, knowing it would be a miracle if we did. A small miracle in the current state of our world, but those small miracles are the exact kind that help your heart know when things are crazy like they had been that He's got it all in His Hands. He's got you and your life in His hands.

Feeling a teeny bit like the parable of the woman searching for the lost coin and a little like this was the perfect 2020 irony, I asked God if I was going to find it or if I should just put it out of mind. I asked Him about puzzles. *"Why puzzles? Is it because everything right now feels like a puzzle?"* A puzzle that doesn't fit together or is missing pieces or is just incomprehensible. Social, political, physical, spiritual, all of it, scrambled about. There is no wonder why putting together a beautiful and complete puzzle feels so calming. *"God, why puzzles? Why me? What about that piece? The whole thing feels cruel and unkind and just like 2020."* At the beginning of the year, I called it the year of glory, the year of double, and while I had experienced snippets of that—confirmations throughout the year in my personal life, and I could feel it in the distance in my surroundings, the big picture didn't reflect that. The whole of 2020 felt disrupted, pain had erupted, and wasn't feeling put together or like it ever could be. New normal is not what I wanted. Old normal was not enough either. I told my Lord the deep questions that I was wrestling with.

"WHY PUZZLES? IS IT BECAUSE EVERYTHING RIGHT NOW FEELS LIKE A PUZZLE?"

I didn't feel like I heard an answer, but I did feel content that I knew He hears me when I speak. 1 Peter says that He is attentive to my prayers (3:12), and I knew that God knew my heart was more concerned about the big picture puzzle and was just annoyed and let down about that actual puzzle piece that was missing. I knew that He would answer me, teach me, and show me just like He always does.

I left my quiet time spot and started to pick up things laying around the house. I opened Ruby's window, helped her make her bed, and started to put away a few things on her floor. Right by her closet, my eye caught a tiny cardboard piece laying face down. Now in our house, you can't get too excited; though it was a puzzle piece, it didn't mean it was the puzzle piece. That girl has all kinds of tiny things she finds and places in her room! To my surprise, but also in my knowing spot—I knew that was my missing puzzle piece! The tiny piece carried off by an unsuspecting foot was not even in the same room as the puzzle! But my God *highlighted* it for me and kept it safe for finding, anyways! *"He guards all that is mine!"* (Psalm 16:5)

Not knowing where that last piece was on the puzzle that I had just spent so many hours working on was not a good feeling. At that moment, I felt foolish to spend my time like that, like I wasn't smart enough to check the bag that the pieces came in well enough. I felt let down, I felt like there was nothing that I could do to resolve it. Sometimes, we find ourselves in spots like that, spots of feeling not enough.

There is a sweet exchange that can take place when we give God our "not enough feelings" and take on His "more than enough ways." The Message Paraphrase puts it this way, *"You're blessed when you're at the end of your rope. With less of you there is more of God and his rule."* (Matthew 5:3) Realization of our fallibility breaks down pride. Pride is something that can so easily creep in spots of our life that we don't even realize it's there; but pride resists God. James 4 tells us that the danger of pride is that God opposes pride. The enemy can use the moments of our frailty to say, "I told you so," or to promote self-loathing or to bring bitter thoughts about ourselves, our situation, or about God and His fairness.

Since the very beginning, the enemy has wanted us to question God's goodness. *"Did God really say, does He even care, or can He even see?"* He is the accuser—the accuser of God, the accuser of Job, the accuser of the brethren. We need to acknowledge this

{ REALIZATION OF OUR FALLIBILITY BREAKS DOWN PRIDE. }

tactic of the accuser to take our questions and give them back to us as doubtful meditations. Then, we can catch ourselves at the start of the "I'm not enough" feelings. Instead of turning towards ourselves and taking great account of all the ways we do not measure up, we can turn towards God who never turns us away and who always has more than enough help! We can, at the end of our rope, find there is more God to behold, to apprehend, and more of God *to rule*. To rule means to take dominion over, to have ultimate authority over.

MORE TO LET HIM RULE

When we are at the end of ourselves; there is more to hand over to God and say, *"God can You take dominion over these areas? I'm not enough here, and I need You. I didn't even realize, I hadn't handed this part over to You yet. These feelings of striving, these feelings of needing to control an area, but God, I need Your ultimate authority right here. God, I am not enough, but You are always more than enough for me!"* Joel 3:10 says, "Let the weak say I am strong!" Paul echoes this in 2 Corinthians 12 when he says, "Therefore I will boast all the more gladly of my weaknesses, so that the power of Christ may rest upon me... For when I am weak, then I am strong." How can we say that too? Because when we posture our heart towards God saying, "I'm at the end of me, I need you," He answers us with, "My grace is sufficient for you, for my power is made perfect in weakness." (2 Corinthians 12:9)

There is more for God to rule! There is more to be handed over to Him. More broken thought patterns. More controlling ways. More pride. More to wash away. And when we hand over our things that we didn't even realize we were holding on to; He puts in our hands treasured moments, treasured words of when I was feeling low, He lifted

{ WHEN WE HAND OVER OUR THINGS THAT WE DIDN'T EVEN REALIZE WE WERE HOLDING ON TO, HE PUTS IN OUR HANDS TREASURED MOMENTS, TREASURED WORDS. }

me. He hands us the missing puzzle piece. He lets us know, He alone, is the Author and the Finisher. He is faithful to complete every good work and He is kind to let us be a part of that good work. Actually, spoiler alert, we *are* the good work! His favorite masterpiece in a galaxy of His magnum opus!

A SEEKING PRAYER

God, thank you that You are so near to us. Thank you that You already know everything that concerns our hearts, whether we have acknowledged those things or not. Thank you for those times where we feel weak, we realize how deeply loved we are, how powerful Your grace is to cover us, and how kind You are to come to us to make all things right. Thank you that You still speak to us in parables and daily life and that You are not a far off God who is not concerned but You care deeply about all the things. Thank you for the little reminders throughout our day that are personal to us. No one has cared for us like You do, because no one knows us as fully as You do, not even ourselves. You see us whole, healed, and finished. You alone know what we need and when we need it. Thank you, for tying up every loose end, finding every missing piece, and thank you for past testimonies of Your goodness. These things build our faith for future miracles and displays of Your kindness! Today our hearts are full of thankfulness because You are good and You are close to us!

A SOAKING SONG

Something Has To Break (by Kierra Sheard) with Red Rocks Worship

CHAPTER SIXTEEN

HOME INSPECTION

One night, I was praying and I kept hearing the thought—*Investigate my heart and test my thoughts and find out if there's any offensive way in me.* I hadn't read this verse recently, and sometimes when I hear a verse, I wonder if I heard it right. I often look up verses in various translations because their unique wordings will hit it differently for me. Sometimes, I get an idea of a verse that was made from a couple of translations merging together in my head so I have to search it out.

"Examine me, God, and know my mind, test me, and know my thoughts."
(Psalm 139:23 ISV)

"Investigate my life, O God, find out everything about me;
Cross-examine and test me."
(Psalm 139: 23 MSG)

I looked up what I was hearing and I realized it was Psalm 139, but I was hearing it in the old Delirious song lyric—"Investigate my life and make me clean, Shine upon the darkest place in me."

While meditating on the words I was hearing, I kept thinking of how investigating is a lot like an inspection. A builder will inspect a home to make sure it's really ready or really good. When buying a home, a home inspection is a part of the process to move forward with getting a loan. It isn't a negotiable part; but it has to happen; and with good reason, because an inspector knows the subtle things to look for that the untrained eye might not see as potential problems. The little things that we don't see or tend to ignore, because they may be under the surface, can have big ramifications if they are left unknown! An inspection can be pricey or time consuming, but what it reveals is very important to know before committing to own or dwell.

I don't know why God speaks to me in Leviticus because when He does, I feel an argument in myself, *"But God, they are going to roll their eyes at me or tune me out. No one wants to hear out of Leviticus."* He must think all the words of the Bible, including Leviticus, are useful because even as I was meditating on inspection, He was bringing to my mind those odd and nauseating Levitical verses about people dealing with bumps and infection. The law, the old covenant, outlined the process that after the person was well, the high priest would come and *inspect the home* to make sure it was really clear and good for the person to return back and rest.

I felt like God was showing me that Jesus is the High Priest under the new covenant. (Hebrews 4) The law of mention, a hermeneutical method for studying the Bible, would instruct us to look at the old high priest to greater our understanding of the new high priest. If the high priest's job was to investigate in the old covenant, then Jesus, as our perfect High Priest, also investigates. King Jesus, honored in the highest place, the One who came to not be served, but to serve and give His life investigating and inspecting our dwelling place, on our behalf. (Matthew 20:28) Jesus, *still* in a hands-on mode with us, is not a far off God on a throne, but a close God in the process, like a builder, he is making sure our foundation is firm with no cracks.

[A CLOSE GOD IN THE PROCESS, LIKE A BUILDER, HE IS MAKING SURE OUR FOUNDATION IS FIRM WITH NO CRACKS.]

In my prayer time, my mind remembered a conversation with a friend earlier that morning. She was telling me that something had happened that she thought she was totally over, but now the feelings were resurfacing and she didn't know why. My heart buzzed, "It's an inspection. Investigate my heart and make me clean."

Jesus is our High Priest and He will, faithfully and perfectly and with kindness, inspect our foundation to see if He sees cracked thoughts or behaviors or whatever. He wants to investigate it with us. Not to us. Not at us. With us. Not like a light in your eyes, harsh inspection of interrogation; but instead as a perfect, loving friend might say, *"Let's sit together and talk about why do we still think this? Let's look at this together."* We really shouldn't feel afraid or dread those times because actually we are spending time together with Jesus and communing with him. We are walking with our friend, Jesus, through the rooms of our soul, the dwelling places of our thoughts and investigating, sifting through anxious cares. This process can feel difficult and exposing, because total transparency is not an easy thing. For who knows a person's thoughts except their own spirit within them? (1 Corinthians 2:11a) Investigation is hard and holy. Hard to the flesh because it is exposed. Holy to the spirit because with full disclosure, grace and mercy rush in and cleanse. Gentle and thoughtful investigation, not being forced *on* us, but *with* Jesus to reveal any wayward cracks that can cause an unsafe and unstable dwelling.

In 2019, we bought our first home! It was a miracle answer to prayer and it is in the beachside community that we've lived and loved for more than ten years. We went through the inspection process and the house was cleared as being solid with a good foundation. For an older beach home built around 60 years ago in the sandy soil of our barrier island, this was a really good report. But wouldn't you know it not long after God gave me this word on inspection, I noticed a gigantic crack on the back corner of our house! Gigantic! I'm talking at least three feet long. These old concrete homes sometimes get a hairline crack here and there and we have seen people in our neighborhood having to repair the stucco or the whole exterior to keep their homes strong; but this corner crack looked very jagged and gapping and was definitely not there, even a few days before.

Sometimes, I feel like, *"God could you spare me the real life examples? I'm listening, I promise."* I'm starting to learn when things like this happen and it's too specific, He is showing me something. And I want you to know that when He shows you something, you want to see! It might be about Him and His character and it's going to be good! You're going to want to see—so lean in, and whatever you do, don't shy away from the scary and unknown!

We called three people to come and inspect the cracked corner. The first said it wasn't a very big problem and they could repair it in an afternoon. The second said a curse word and asked us if we were sure that it hadn't been hit by something big. He shook his head, but said he could fix it. I have to admit, my confidence wasn't there so I called a third, well-recommended person, who knew his stuff. He said he could repair it and had seen a lot of that lately and he was very busy. Days and days went by and he never called back!

I felt frustrated and told God, *"We need direction! None of these people know what they are talking about or if they do, they aren't getting back to us. And God, it's the season in Florida where it rains every afternoon, we need direction!"* I don't know about you, but in our lives, it doesn't seem we have the luxury of focusing on one big problem at a time. This was in the middle of the pandemic, the middle of standing in the gap for someone we love very much who was having foundational issues in the heart, and it appeared like the actual back of our house was falling off. Not trying to be dramatic, but life feels dramatic sometimes! When my cares are piling up and I don't know what to do, something that has been helpful for me is this—when accusation or doubt or fear comes knocking at my door. I mentally pull it into court, with God as Judge, and I stand the doubt or fear before Him and ask God, *"What do you say?"*

God, this person is speaking threats. God what do You say?
God, I have no idea how we will be able to cover these bills?
God, these people who I trust, who are my friends, are all saying I am wrong, I need to know what do You say?
God, our house looks like it is actually crumbling, what do You say?

And when I hear His answer—**it brings order.**

Every time I sought the Lord, He answered me. In 2 Samuel 22, David says *"I sought the Lord in my distress and I called out to Him and from His holy temple He heard my voice and my cry came up to his ears!"*

And I heard His answer:
"Did I not give you this house? Do I not guard all that is yours? Would I perform miracle after miracle concerning this house, to give you a bad gift? What father among you, if his son asks for a fish, will give him a snake instead of a fish? If you...know how to give good gifts to your children, how much more will your heavenly Father give the Holy Spirit to those who ask and continue to ask Him!" (Luke 11)

His answers bring order to your thoughts and comfort to your mind. *When my anxieties multiply, your comforting calms me down.* (Psalm 94:19 CEB) While I still didn't have an answer to what was going on with the house, I had the comfort of knowing God gave me the house. He guards all that's mine—all that's His. In return, I chose to give my house and my whole life to His care.

We still weren't really sure what to do about the crack. Anthony woke up one morning and told me that in a dream he was looking through our house papers from the previous owner. He felt like we needed to look through them again. We had many distractions at that moment and we both completely forgot about the dream and the house papers. A few mornings later, when I was frustratedly asking God for direction, He faithfully brought the house papers to my mind. I went to our files and found some documents about foundation work that had been done to our house 19 years prior.

The documents outlined a problem with our house settling because of poor, sandy soil and explained that in this condition, if left untouched, would cause settling and great damage to the house. Apparently, our house had gone under an extensive and expensive process to firm up and support the soil and this work was guaranteed for 25 years. Then, I found another letter from the same company, in the previous year, explaining that the house had been inspected and the previous foundation repairs were doing their job and there was no active settling. The letter was dated just weeks before we ever saw the house and made an offer to purchase it!

I immediately thanked the Holy Spirit for guiding us to these papers! There was an active warranty and the company was still in business! The next thing I did was call my prayer partner and tell her about my situation. She said, "Brooke, what is God teaching you about foundations? He is telling you something; it's definitely something deeper and He is speaking it only to you!" When she said this, the Holy Spirit brought to my mind a dream that I had about soil just two weeks prior!

In that dream, there was a neighbor who had done a lot of great work on their house. They replaced the driveway, painted the house, and sodded their yard with plush beautiful grass. We were taking a walk and Anthony stopped us. He said, "Oh no! They just did all this work on this house, and spent all this money on this grass like we want to do, but they messed up!" I said, "What? It looks great." Anthony said, "Look underneath it," then he pulled the corner up and there was dry, sandy, rocky dirt. He said, "They didn't till or prepare the ground; it's never gonna grow well. Look, the bags of soil are right there in the driveway. Why didn't they use them? Did they forget it's crucial to have good soil for what they plant to take root and grow? We need to tell them; we could help them save it! It has to be done soon, right away."

The foundation needs to be inspected, but God is also teaching me that the soil affects the foundation. Cracks in our foundation can be caused by a settling that results from poor or loose soil. Jesus told us about the house needing to be built on the rock, the words of His Father, and to not be like the house built on the sand, for when the rains and storms came, it fell and had a great fall. (Matthew 7)

My Florida house had displayed its strength by withstanding many hurricanes, even one the previous year. The house had a great foundation, inspection approved, but because of the nature of the soil it was built on, the soil also needed to be supported and inspected. This must be part of the trade off of living on the beach. Since I knew without doubt that God called my family to this beach community, then I also knew He was going to help us navigate the process to keep our foundation, figuratively and literally, strong and supported.

Inspection of the house matters, but inspection of the soil matters too. If you examine the world that we have been given to build God's Kingdom, it can look a lot like my situation. *"But God, it's sandy, unstable; have you seen the world out there?"* We might not get to choose where we build, but we can diligently sift and support the soil so that our foundation remains stable. Is our foundation built on every word that is spoken on social media or the news or is it on every Word that comes from the mouth of God? Who gets the final say? What gets to stay under our foundation? If your soil is weak because of its mixed up nature, it's time to stabilize the weak spots to support what you've built.

> IS OUR FOUNDATION BUILT ON EVERY WORD THAT IS SPOKEN ON SOCIAL MEDIA OR THE NEWS, OR IS IT ON EVERY WORD THAT COMES FROM THE MOUTH OF GOD? WHO GETS THE FINAL SAY?

Let me put it this way, if everywhere you place your attention is full of fear, casuality, passivity, and lacks direction; you have to purposefully stabilize your gaze with—the Word of God, hope, good news, positive relationships, passion—all the good stuff to help support and align your foundational beliefs about God, yourself, and your situation. Are these the keys or answers on their own? No, only the Word of God is without fail, but there are good dividends when you add those strategic strengths that the Word of God supports.

It is crucial that your foundation is firm so that God can build whatever He desires—relationships, ministries, the entire Kingdom person that you are! The foundation must be strong because it is meant to be built upon. Don't focus solely on the foundation of your beliefs while discounting the environment you're in. The soil of your surroundings needs to be examined too because it is ever changing. We have to stabilize and imbed the rock, the Cornerstone beneath the foundation. This makes me think of Peter, in Matthew 16, when Jesus asked the disciples,

"Who do people say that the Son of Man is?" And they said, "Some say John the Baptist, others say Elijah, and others Jeremiah or one of the prophets." He said to them, "But who do you say that I am?" Simon Peter replied, "You are the Christ, the Son of the living God." And Jesus answered him, "Blessed are you, Simon Bar-Jonah! For flesh and blood has not revealed this to you, but my Father who is in heaven. And I tell you, you are Peter, and on this rock, I will build my church, and the gates of hell shall not prevail against it. I will give you the keys of the kingdom of heaven, and whatever you bind on earth shall be bound in heaven, and whatever you loose on earth shall be loosed in heaven." (Matthew 16: 15-19)

On this rock, on this foundation, petra, the church, the ekklésía is built. Ekklésía, what we call the church, means those belonging to God, those with one heart—the bride of Christ. All that we build must rest on the foundation of faith that Jesus is the son of God, the Savior of the world, the Savior of our lives every day, no matter the situation. He is for us and for our good—this is our Cornerstone. He is our Cornerstone. Apart from Him, there is no good.

Do you know what happens if the soil is left in it's weakened state? There will be a settling in the foundation. Not settle, like we talked about before, where you are stubbornly settled into the care of God; but a sinking in, a compromising state, a giving way, or shrinking back. If our soil is allowed to remain weak, it will compromise everything built upon it. Slowly, we will sink in so mildly and gradually that we won't even notice until there is a gaping crack needing attention.

The two main causes of this kind of settling are weather and time. The storms of life will challenge our foundation and can change our soil's makeup. What you built upon twenty years ago may no longer be the same conditions under your foundation. As the temperament of your world changes, you need to add support to stabilize areas that have

> WINDS, RAINS, AND STORMS WILL CHALLENGE A PHYSICAL FOUNDATION AND MEDIA, ENTERTAINMENT, POLITICS AND SOCIAL ISSUES WILL CHALLENGE A SPIRITUAL ONE.

been affected by the environment. Winds, rains, and storms will challenge a physical foundation and media, entertainment, politics and social issues will challenge a spiritual one. Examine what areas may need structural support because if your environment is like mine, it is a mix of good and weak soil.

Time will also challenge your foundation. We can't rely on the notion that we simply know about God, that we are a good person, or that everything is fine and there is nothing to be searched out. Over time we can become apathetic if we aren't actively searching our thoughts to make sure they are aligned with God's Word. Without frequent inspection and stabilization, time and weather cause slow, almost unnoticeable compromise to the soil under our foundation.

The same Peter of Matthew 16 later on calls believers "living stones" that are built on Christ as the foundation and cornerstone. (1 Peter 2:5-6) We are the living stones with the words of our testimony that Jesus cares for us, He knows us, and is involved in our lives. We renew our minds when we remember our testimony of walking with God! We have to remember who we are talking about. We are talking about *Jesus*. He is not a far off, distant God; but He is close and a friend. He is the cornerstone, the center of it all. Jesus is our High Priest, our faithful Inspector, and we can take great comfort in Him because we know Him! We know His ways and everything that He does concerning us is for our good!

INVESTIGATE

Invite the investigating gaze of the High Priest in your life. Allow Jesus to sit with you and look at the inner parts of your life—your thoughts and your beliefs. What comes out when pressed? Ask Him for guidance. Let Him look at your outer life. Are the parts that the world sees true? How is the environment affecting your foundation? Sit with your friend, Jesus, and invite Him to address anything that He wants to. You don't have to feel scared with Him. You can have complete assurance in Him.

A SEEKING PRAYER

Oh, Jesus, I invite You to investigate my foundation and my environment! My High Priest, search through my life, like the old Delirious song says, "To You my life is an open book, turn the pages and take a look." Jesus, search me and know my thoughts. Help me, that I may not compromise, that I may not settle, that I may not shrink back. Help me to have a confident faith, help me build eternally. Jesus, I'm not trying to do it alone; let your Holy Spirit guide me, strengthen me, and stabilize me. It is You who heals, it is You who makes every stumbling way divinely healed! (Hebrews 12) Inspect my heart and make me new!

A SOAKING SONG
Investigate by Delirious / Spotlight by Rita Springer

CHAPTER SEVENTEEN

STOREHOUSE OF TREASURES

He responded, "Every scholar of the Scriptures, who is instructed in the
ways of heaven's kingdom realm, is like a wealthy homeowner with his
house filled with treasures both new and old. And he knows how and
when to bring them out to show others."
(Matthew 13:52 TPT)

Many words of comfort, faith, and peace that God has given me came in the darkest of nights. Even though some of the harder situations I would have never wanted, these times revealed to me the treasure of knowing a God who knows, sees, and speaks in every circumstance! His words have filled the rooms of my heart. Now I have both treasures that are new, as well as old precious ones gained from walking with Him through many seasons of life. I like the Passion translation of this passage, "He knows how and when to bring them out to show others." For me, that is how this book has come about.

God gently impressed on my heart that now is that time to share some of my hard fought battles and perspectives. These treasures came from sitting in the secret place and asking, *"God what do you say?"* then hearing my beloved Father answer me. He didn't just speak; He filled me with His Word. He didn't just fill me with His Word; He surrounded me with His Presence and He imparted courage.

> HE DIDN'T JUST FILL ME WITH HIS WORD; HE SURROUNDED ME WITH HIS PRESENCE AND HE IMPARTED COURAGE.

Proverbs 31:15 says, "Even in the night season she arises and sets food on the table for hungry ones in her house and for others." My night seasons gave me words that I feel are not just for me, but for my children and for others. Jesus tells us that words are sustenance. Jesus answered, "It is written: 'Man shall not live by bread alone, but by every word that comes from the mouth of God.'" (Matthew 4:4) A Word from God helps us live life abundantly and with victory! His precious words and His nearness helps us identify as children of God and take up our places in the Kingdom as mediators and intercessors.

There is such purpose found in the night seasons because they yield treasure to the one who has ears to hear, eyes to see, and a mind to conceive. If we can grab hold of the treasures in darkness—the secret riches, and the biggest treasure of all, knowing it is God who calls our name, (Isaiah 45:3) then we will walk into the new day with a new authority and perspective that our God will come through just as He said. He's never lost a battle and He's never left us forsaken. In Jewish tradition, the day actually begins at sunset. If we take up our position in the night; watching and waiting on the Lord, how might it influence our day? Remember, His yoke is easy and light. The night watch, the darkness, can be a time of resting in the knowledge of Him and recovering strength. His yoke is *light*. His yoke is light in weight, but it also is the very light that will drive away the darkness.

Yes, the dark seasons always pass and lead to better days, my friend. I pray that the treasures you uncover in darkness are stored up in your storehouse. I hope that you know that when you need them, you can examine these treasures you've uncovered and encourage yourself in the Lord by what He spoke to you. To encourage means to give courage. I pray that you know deep down, you can share these treasures and they will literally give courage to others!

Treasures from night seasons fill the rooms of your heart with gems and spoils of old wars. They enlarge your faith with visions of new treasures yet to be yours! At the end of that difficult year of breathing battles and loss of friends from death and moving away, I read a book called *Raising Burning Hearts* by Patricia Bootsma that

> TREASURES FROM NIGHT SEASONS FILL THE ROOMS OF YOUR HEART WITH GEMS AND SPOILS OF OLD WARS.

inspired Anthony and I to create a family decree for our children. Biblically, a decree is praying in line with the will of God. We prayed and asked God to give us some scriptures for our family, then together we created a decree that we say over our children each day. Each night we pray with them:

You have a faith that moves mountains, a call that is unshakable, an identity that is sured up in Christ—you are a child of God. You are creative and gifted and will glorify God with your talents. You are a lover of God's presence. You know God's voice and He knows yours. You are a generous giver and a blessing to everyone you meet. You have the favor of God and are wise beyond your years. You have a purity that is unquestionable and will only marry the one that God has for you. You walk in righteousness, joy and peace overflowing in the Holy Spirit. You have protection and provision everywhere you go. Surely, goodness and mercy will follow you all the days of your life.

Anthony and I based our family decree on prayers of scripture with hope and desire for our children to know that every day God is *with* them, *for* them, and has a plan for *their future*—and that plan is for their good! When we renovated the house that God gave us, we wrote the decree on the slab foundation before we laid the flooring. It has been a foundational prayer that our family treasures!

When your storehouses are filled with words that God has spoken to your heart and cherished memories of when He came through for you again and again, it gives you hope for the future! You no longer are praying only about what you are going through now, you are praying into your future and for others—praying promises of scripture. Your faith has grown because of the revelation of God. Jesus said, "To you it has been given to know the secrets of the kingdom of heaven, but to them it has not been given. For to the one who has, more will be given, and he will have an abundance, but from the one who has not, even what he has will be taken away." (Matthew 13) If you've been given revelation of His words and you hold onto them, He will give you more! Jesus cautions that if we don't have revelation, then we will end up with even less. That's why reflecting on

His words matters. We receive actual reflections of Heaven's perspectives, which influences our worldviews. If we are careful to reflect on His Word, He promises there will be more and more!

COSTLY TREASURE

Revelation 3 is a special passage to me and in verse 18, Jesus tells the church, "Buy from me gold refined by the fire." Treasures that were purified in intensity. Riches hidden in the secret place and meditating on the Word. Oh, that He desires we purchase gold *from* Him. This treasure is so costly. It is not cheap or too delicate to go through fire. It is firm and can stand in opposition of fear. Treasure comes from our Beloved, who has never left us or refused us, but has purified us by fire and taught us the ways of endurance by holding our hand. We hold on to what we have learned as gold; and we walk in the footsteps as ones who have been tried by fire and came out holy. His treasured words remain in us and the sword of His Spirit comes with authority out of our mouths. "So I counsel you to purchase gold perfected by fire, so that you can be truly rich. Purchase a white garment to cover and clothe your shameful Adam-nakedness. Purchase eye salve to be placed over your eyes so that you can truly see. All those I dearly love I unmask and train." (Revelation 3:18-19 TPT) In the raw and open places, we were unmasked and became eager to pursue what is right.

It is the most costly of treasures, but it is so worth it. The world could never produce such treasure and so many are left seeking in all the wrong places and wind up empty handed. Only those who are willing to buy gold refined by fire understand the cost—to live abiding in God's Presence and be aware of Him relationally means that you have to consider things more. You have to consider their worth. Often it means to take a hard and holy path. Sometimes it feels like *others may and you may not*. It may seem as if it will be lonely, but when you are alone—you are gaining alone time with God. It feels like lonely times which are better called "alone with Him times," will stay, but they don't! Life picks up again and you'll have to fight to have your times of quiet. Treasure time with just God.

"Behold, I'm standing at the door, knocking. If your heart is open to hear
my voice and you open the door within, I will come in to you and feast
with you, and you will feast with me."
(Revelation 3:20)

He will always be there and Jesus tells us that if we hear His voice (His words), we will feast because He has prepared a table for us! Psalm 23:5 says, "A table before my enemies!" Remember, Luke 14 speaks about the master who prepared a feast that others refused to be a part of, who sent his servant to go out into the highways and along the hedges, and compel the needy to come to his prepared feast! Don't miss it. Hear His voice, and open the door within.

"I overflow with praise when I come before you,
for the anointing of your presence satisfies me like nothing else.
You are such a rich banquet of pleasure to my soul.

I lie awake each night thinking of you
and reflecting on how you help me like a father."
(Psalm 63:5-6 TPT)

In times of darkness, you've become acquainted with the One who wants to dine with you. The One who helps you like a Father. If that's not enough, Jesus says, "And to the one who conquers I will give the privilege of sitting with me on my throne, just as I conquered and sat down with my Father on his throne. The one whose heart is open let him *listen carefully to what the Spirit is saying now to the churches.*" (Revelation 3:21 TPT, emphasis mine)

He sees you as a conquering champion and perhaps in darkness, you've grown to realize this about yourself too. "In all these things we are more than conquerors and gain an overwhelming victory through Him who loved us [so much that He died for us]." (Romans 8:38 AMP) How wild is this love that He has not only given you the treasures of His words, but He also sees *you* as His treasured possession?

"But you are God's chosen treasure—priests who are kings, a spiritual 'nation'
set apart as God's devoted ones. He called you out of darkness to experience
his marvelous light, and now he claims you as his very own. He did this so that
you would broadcast his glorious wonders throughout the world."
(1 Peter 2:8 TPT)

TESTIMONY OF TREASURE

Your treasured words become the testimony of your Beloved Identity and show others the way to revelation! Because you are God's chosen treasure, they too can become God's chosen treasure. Because you have been set free from darkness, they too can be set free! There is such purpose in the treasure of the words that God gives you. You can be like that wealthy homeowner with his house filled with treasures *both new and old.* You can know how and when to bring them out to show others. The world needs to know! We can be a bridge for others by broadcasting His glorious wonders. Friend, I pray that this book has shown you that no matter how small or how grand, no matter if it was read, spoken, or perceived—that God is always speaking. Tune your heart to listen—He will answer you. He does care and He is not distant; but is so close. You were created to know Him and you can hear His words. You don't have to become a better person or do a list of things. It is in the fibers of who you are—you were created to be able to connect with God.

If somehow you're at the end of this book and still don't have a relationship with Jesus, I want you to know it's as easy as inviting Him into your heart and to be Lord of your life. Posture your heart and ask Him to forgive you of sin and for following the ways of the world. Invite Him into your life and let Him know that now your life belongs to Him and you'll follow His leading. You want to learn to hear His Words and to have a thriving relationship with Him. Next, I would encourage you to tell somebody! We overcome, both our past and our future, by what Jesus did for us and by the word of our testimony! If you don't have anyone to tell, tell me—*brookerickwrites@gmail.com.* I would love to know!

If you do have a relationship with God, I hope that you feel the Holy Spirit inspiring you! I hope that there is a strong desire rising up so that you want to go back and take account of every time that you have heard the treasure of God's words and knew He was speaking to you! Grab a notebook and make it your treasure trove of all your revelations and all your God-secrets that God has spoken straight to you. Just like I encourage our new friends in Christ—tell somebody! We don't have to be afraid to speak what we hear. Words *are* treasures! And God has an unlimited supply of treasure, specifically, for you.

A SEEKING PRAYER

Thank you Jesus for filling the storehouses of our hearts with treasures of past provisions and past answers of love. Your Word is our source of hope! The riches of Your words give us eyes to believe that we will see you move again and again for our good. Not just for our good, but to bring your Kingdom on Earth as it is in Heaven. Thank you for walking with us through every season. Thank you for never leaving us or getting impatient with us. You are so, so kind.

Jesus, I pray that the words of my treasures spark hope in the heart of every reader. Show them that you care about the small things just as much as the big things, and that you desire for them to know you and hear your voice.

Holy Spirit, breathe on us, rest on us, and empower us to boldly broadcast your glory with our very lives!

A SOAKING SONG
Midnight by Rita Springer

ACKNOWLEDGEMENTS

This book was conceived in my heart long before it ever made it to paper. I'm very thankful for the people who spoke life over this project when it was still in the processing stage, and those who read the rough, rough drafts.

Anthony, you encouraged me when I felt inadequate and reminded me that I do have something to say. You allowed me time, space, and if they were awake, kept the kids happy when I was writing. Anthony, you believed in me and validated me when I've been in this behind the scenes role of ministry and motherhood. Thank you for choosing the costly things with me. This book is a product of the rest in our home and that is a rest you fiercely protect. This book is as much yours as it is mine because without you it would not be. I will love you for all of my days.

Silas Gage, at youth camp one summer the speaker was talking about identity and it was a really serious moment and the room full of teens had started sniffling, you looked over to me and with a big smile said, "I know who I am—a cool, fun, Jesus loving guy!" It is my prayer for all your days you feel just like that! I'm so honored to be your mom and I love you so much! You are so brave, so cool, and so you. I love you, Si- guy!

Ezra Arrow, my wild child. You do have a faith that moves mountains and a conviction that we say is like John the Baptist. You are so passionate and I love that about you. You are not too much but exactly what the world needs. I love how fierce you are, but also how compassionate and tender. You slay and war but you cuddle and need may-may too. Ezra, I love you!

Ruby Autumn, my gem! You are sweet, sensitive, and you are strong. You are the best little friend and my partner. You are your daddy's little bird. Before you were even in my belly, God gave me a dream about a beautiful little girl named Ruby. It's so special to me because I was just learning to hear and believe that I heard. I thought you would look just like Silas but right before you were born, I had another dream and your complexion was light and you had loose, curly hair the color of Ezra's. Ruby, you are my dream come true. I love you, Roo!

Mom, thank you for answering every call. There have been a lot of them. You are my best friend, my prayer partner, my vault. You know my secrets and you believe and pray with me. Most people don't know the brave contender you are, but I do, and heaven does. I am so thankful for you and I want to be a woman of prayer and faith just like you.

Dad, you are the very best dad ever. I know you're not perfect, but to me you are exactly what I need. I feel like I had the greatest dad and that gave me no limitations when I ran to God, the Father. I'm so thankful that you always put God first in our family. Now you are the world's best Papi and I am so thankful that my kids get to have you. You're the best!

Alyssa, you've been my best friend since 1990. Thank you for all the times you helped me not lose my mind. Thank you for being all in with me even with all the feelings. You really get me and love me and you are such a gift. I love that you're my sister. You get your entirely own category.

Austin, I feel like I should just write this to my bro. You have become one of my best friends. Who would have thought? It really shows that redemption is the sweetest gift. I feel like you have taught me all of the years of our ministry. You taught me who I was to reach. Your life showed me what they actually needed. You taught me that it has to be real and we can't fake it. You made me look hard at myself and ask if I was faking it. You taught by example the purity of being a seeker, the beauty of c onsecration, and the joys of peace. I remember looking at you and knowing that is what I want. I still look at you and see that. I can't even wait to see what is next. You're at the doorway!

Pastor Jason, I'm so thankful that Anthony and I have grown under your leadership and example. You haven't just taught us the easy things but you've shown us what it means to walk through the hard things even when everyone wants to comment. I am so thankful to be one of the ones who can say I saw the fruit even when it looked like a mess. You really are a hero to us. And you're a real one and that makes it even better! Sorry, for when I made a grocery list one time when you were preaching...I've grown a little bit since then, haha.

Raina Byars, you've been teaching me all along...like the year you didn't have a cell phone so you could be intentional with your children or how you love your husband and marriage like it's the best thing that's ever happened. I would watch you intentionally stay in that vibe day after day. You taught me, by example, how to love the Word of God, how to not just listen to it sometimes, or to say, "oh, I know that verse," but how to treasure it! You've also taught me how to not give up when it definitely would've been easier to live on a private island, content that you gave some of your best years. I see how you hold onto the visions that God has given and how you do it for the Kingdom.

Paige Lawson, thank you for always wondering with me! What a gift for a feeler like me. We've been friends through all of this and you've known the depths of these moments.

Brianna Price, you are my friend who has always held me accountable. "You are not hanging out, why? Why are you not writing already?" You really are a cheer-leader and you've been my agent for years, haha!

Gerri Rick, my mother-in-love, you bless me in many ways and you were one of the first to read and help me edit. It was such a big deal to me. Thank you for loving me the way you do.

I'm thankful for Anthony's grandma, Betty Johnson, for telling me that I have to write while she is still alive, and for my grandma, Betty Hoskins, who lets me know that it is a gift to be able to communicate with words.

I am especially full of gratitude to Laura Fadden who treasured this project with me! Her expertise helped turn my writings into a book that could be shared with others. It was the biggest gift to me, not just your talent and time, but that you believed in me! You are one of the best friends that I have ever had and I am so thankful for you. I can't even begin to count the reasons. I love you, Laura!

Maddie Ryan is the artist who designed the beautiful lettering and art on the cover. What a gift she has!

The family photograph is the amazing work of Danielle Marie Photography. It's one of my favorites!

Thank you, thank you, I wouldn't have been brave enough without all of you.

Made in the USA
Columbia, SC
23 September 2021